CW00376886

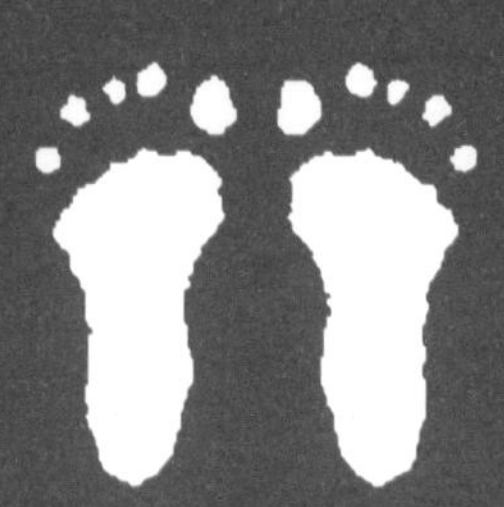

The Barefoot Book of

HEROES

The Barefoot Book of

HEROES

Written and Illustrated by Rebecca Hazell

BAREFOOT BOOKS
BATH

Contents

V=(2e/h)V

For Chögyam Trungpa Mukpo, friend, teacher and hero, who taught me what heroism is.

Barefoot Collections
an imprint of
Barefoot Books
PO Box 95
Kingswood
Bristol
BS30 5BH

First published in Great Britain in 1997 by Barefoot Books Ltd. This edition printed in 1999.

Graphic design by Design/Section, Frome
Printed and bound in Hong Kong by South China Printing Co. (1988) Ltd
This book has been printed on 100% acid-free paper

Hardcover ISBN 1 898000 38 7
Paperback ISBN 1 84148 201 3

British Cataloguing-in-Publication Data: a catalogue record for this book is available from the British Library

3 5 7 9 8 6 4 2

Acknowledgements

Thank you to my husband, Mark, and children, Elisabeth and Stephan, for all their support and patience. Again, thanks to the many friends who contributed books and ideas to this project. A special thanks goes to the librarians of Halifax, in particular those of Captain William Spry Library, who went out of their way to be helpful. Last but not least, thanks go to my mother, Doris Knotts, to my publisher, Tessa Strickland, and to Kate Parker and Meredith Wolf, my tireless and thorough copy-editors.

Introduction

Did you ever wish you could visit faraway places or travel in time? You can do these things every time you open a history book. History is the story of people like you and me, leading colourful lives and having adventures.

Most history books only tell about governments, wars and treaties and dates. Of course these are important, but if you're like me, you want to imagine what it felt like to live in a world quite different from our own. That's how I have tried to write this book, which is about some of the people in history who led lives that have been very special in some way. You might think of heroes as brave leaders, fearless warriors, daring rescuers, or even sports champions. My idea of a hero is not limited to these kinds of people. I think a hero is anyone who is brave, kind or wise – not just once, but throughout his life.

You will find all kinds of heroes in this book, from all around the world and from different periods of history. Some were great warriors or rulers, and others were artists, scientists, authors and philosophers. All of them did things that still affect us today. These men made mistakes like anyone else does, and some of them had talents that were not properly recognised in their day. But they all used their talents to the full, living their lives with courage and conviction.

Of course there were (and are) many more heroes than could fit into these pages. There are heroes – and heroines – living all over the world, and many of them will never be famous. There just isn't room for everyone in one book.

I have tried to illustrate each hero just as someone living in his time might have. I hope that, when you read this book, it will make you think of heroes of your own, inspiring you to use your own special talents to be heroic in your own way.

Rebecca Hazell

Socrates

About 2400 years ago, a stonemason named Socrates began a quest for truth. He lived in the Greek city-state of Athens. As a young man, Socrates bravely served his city as part of its volunteer army. Once his fellow soldiers found him standing immovable by his tent. For many hours, they could do nothing to break his strange concentration.

He never told anyone what had happened to him then, but when his war duties were over, he began to question why the world exists. Finally, he stopped working and began studying. He looked into science for answers, but without success. He wanted to know more than how things worked; he wanted to know the purpose of life. Since everyone had a different answer to his question, he decided to find his own answers.

Socrates began by asking himself what people are like. He saw that everyone wanted happiness. He also saw that people mistakenly believed pleasure, power or success would make them happy, even though many who had these things were unhappy. He concluded that until they found what was true and good, they could not be happy. This meant searching within themselves to separate the false from the true. To Socrates, the purpose of life and the way to happiness was to find and live the truth.

As he grew older, Socrates spent his days at the market-place chatting with people: young men, politicians or other philosophers. At that time, the market-place was where ideas as well as goods were exchanged. Students came there to learn about wisdom from travelling teachers. Through his conversations with people, Socrates became known as the wisest man of his day. He asserted that he knew only that he did not know, while others pretended to wisdom they didn't really have.

Socrates' motto was: 'The unexamined life is not worth living.' Taking nothing on faith, he inquired into each person's beliefs. Through logic and with humour, he helped them see what they did not know, so they could recognise truth for themselves. He questioned anyone and everyone in this way. Unfortunately, some people did not want their opinions questioned. Athens had been a great power in Greece when Socrates was young, but by the time he was an old man wars, plague and political unrest troubled the city. Socrates made many enemies with his ceaseless questions. Angry politicians arrested him, charging him with demoralising young people and slandering the gods. They thought he would escape to another city, be discredited and stop bothering them.

ΣΟΚΡΑΤΗΣ

Socrates knew that if he was arrested, he would be tried and convicted by a frightened mob. Yet if he ran away, he would betray both his beloved Athens and his own teachings about living the truth. Instead of fleeing, he chose to stay and face his certain penalty: death.

The way in which Socrates accepted his death immortalised him. Two of his students, Plato and Xenophon, wrote famous descriptions of his life, his teaching method and his courageous end. Even today, he is remembered for his humour and integrity, while his pursuit of truth became the foundation for Western philosophy.

All Greeks idealised the heroic warrior; Socrates gave them the ideal of the heroic philosopher.

THE BRIEF GLORY OF ATHENS

Ancient Greece was not one united country but a series of little city-states that ruled over their local countryside. These city-states shared the same language and worshipped the same gods, but each had a different form of government. Citizens of each city-state were deeply loyal to their community and suspicious of other city-states.

Then, around 505 BC, Athens developed a form of government known as direct democracy. Rather than electing representatives, its citizens (excluding women, slaves and foreigners) could vote directly about what they wanted Athens to do. For a while, this kind of government worked well for those who could vote, but Athenian democracy ran into some big problems.

Difficulties arose after the great empire of Persia invaded Greece around 490 BC. The Greek city-states always had a hard time getting along with each other and were only able to form an alliance when threatened. Together they fought bravely against the Persian invaders, but after Athens led them to final victory in 449 BC, the other city-states resented Athens' leadership. They had good reason, for Athens soon slipped into imperialism. Originally the other city-states had contributed to a treasury for their common defence. The leaders of Athens seized this money (called tributes) under the pretence that they were in danger of invasion; then they began demanding tributes.

While Athens prospered, its voters were happy. They re-elected the same leader, Pericles, again and again. Pericles had a great vision for his city. He wanted it to lead Greece in peace as well as war, to be a centre for culture and art. After the Persian wars were over, he set its craftsmen and artists to work creating great public monuments and temples. The grandest and most beautiful was the Parthenon, dedicated to Athens' patron goddess, Athena. Socrates probably helped build it. At the same time, drama, poetry, philosophy and science flourished. Athens did become the centre of Greek culture, but at the expense of its neighbours – their tributes paid for it.

The Parthenon – standing on top of the massive hill known as the Acropolis – contained a gigantic statue of Athena, goddess of wisdom.

This 'golden age' could not last. Led by Athens' old rival, Sparta, the other city-states took their revenge. Athens' power slowly crumbled as it had to face repeated invasions and sieges, plus plague and famine. At this point, its democracy crumbled, too. No one could agree on how to defend the city properly. The people were easily swayed by any convincing speaker. Fear, not good sense, lay behind their votes. Twice, small groups of powerful men used their private armies to take over the government and terrorise their own people. By the time democracy was restored, Athens had changed. Its citizens no longer welcomed freedom of thought. They wanted security instead.

The elderly Socrates became the victim of this new mentality. His style of questioning had been abused by some of his students, and two former students had actually betrayed Athens during its time of upheaval. Socrates understood the fear people felt. He knew it made them weak. At his trial, he refused to rely on grandiose speeches or to beg for pity in order to sway their emotions. Instead he told them that he had been Athens' gadfly of truth, whose questioning roused its citizens out of their stupidity and greed. Expecting to be condemned by all, he did actually sway his jurors – he was condemned by only a narrow majority.

COURAGE TO THE END

It was Athenian tradition to ask a condemned man what his punishment should be. At the end of Socrates' trial, he answered that instead of being punished, he should be given free dinners for the rest of his life! His lack of seriousness angered the voters, and they gave him the death sentence. There was no appeal.

While he awaited his execution, Socrates' friends urged him to escape. They offered to bribe his gaoler, but he refused to leave. First, he knew he would be discredited. Also he believed in obeying Athens' laws, even when they were unjust. He was certain that his death would be more of a gift to his community than living longer, as through it his integrity would be preserved.

In the meantime, his friends would visit him and continue to discuss philosophy and the meaning of life. When the day came for Socrates to die, his gaolers gave him a poisoned drink made from hemlock root. He drank it without hesitating. Surrounded by weeping friends, Socrates talked calmly as the poison took effect. He found himself comforting them until he died.

One of his students, Plato, described not only Socrates' passing but also his life in a series of question-and-answer dialogues. Plato later became as famous as his teacher. No one is quite sure whether Plato's biography tells us more about Socrates' philosophy or his own, but what Plato did make clear was how wise, courageous, humorous and beloved he had been. Socrates remained loyal to his community to the end. Perhaps he foresaw that it would someday extend beyond Athens to include all seekers of wisdom.

GREECE IN THE 6TH–4TH CENTURIES BC

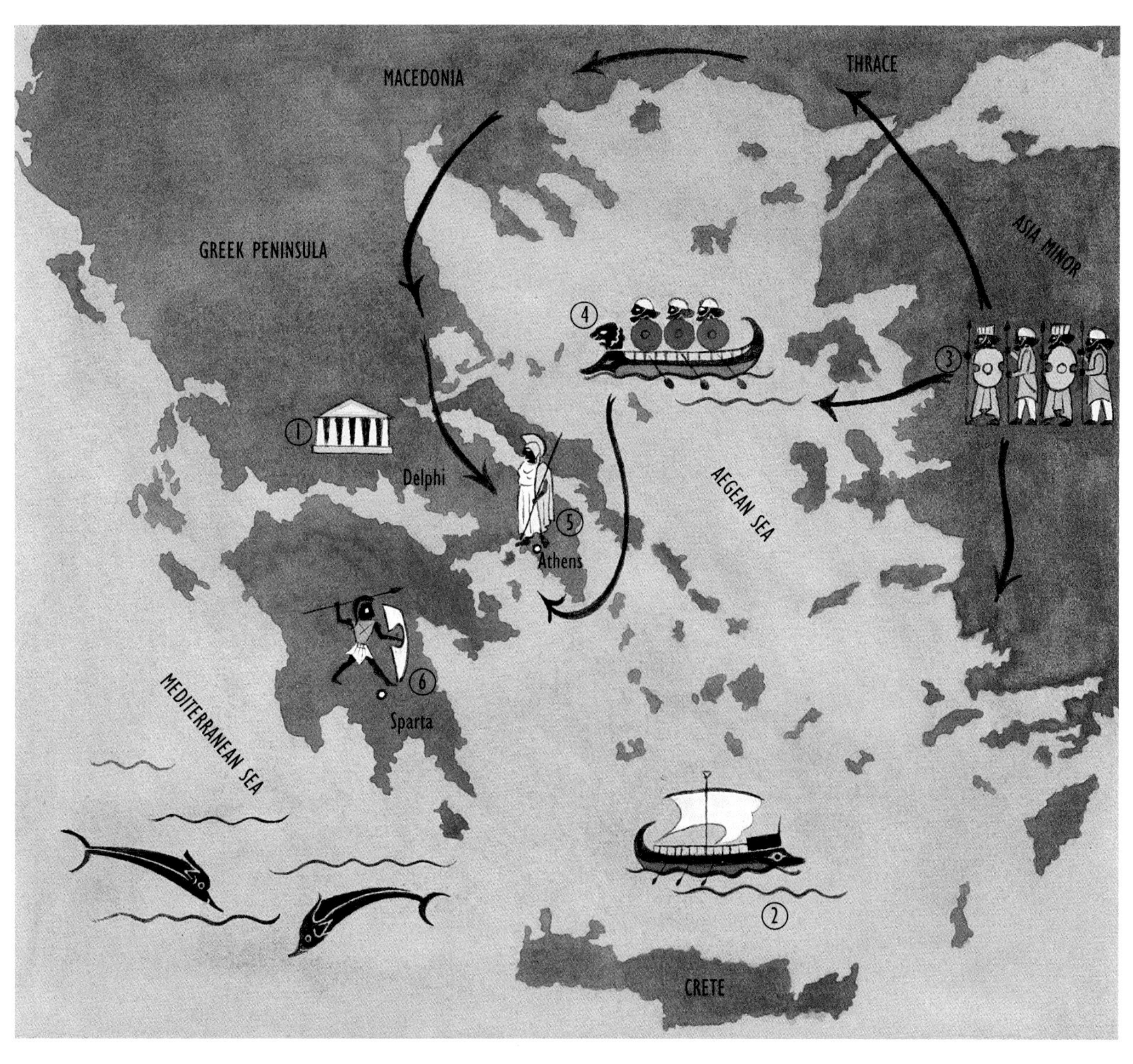

1. In ancient Greece, one of the major religious shrines was at Delphi, where a priestess delivered oracles.
2. The ancient Greeks populated many islands in the Aegean and Mediterranean seas, had colonies in Italy and Asia Minor and traded with other countries along the coast of the Mediterranean.
3. In the late sixth century BC, the mighty Persian Empire conquered the Greek cities in Asia Minor, followed by Thrace, Macedonia and finally Greece itself.
4. Persia twice tried to conquer Greece, but the little city-states combined forces, managing to defeat the huge Persian navy.
5. The Persians had burned Athens, yet the city not only survived complete destruction but, after being rebuilt, emerged more beautiful than ever.
6. Sparta led the other city-states in defeating Athens, bringing to an end a 'golden age' for the arts in ancient Greece.

 Prince Taishi Shotoku 

Thirteen hundred years ago, Japan was a rustic island 'empire' on the edge of Asia. Its rulers claimed to be descended from their sun goddess, Amaterasu. But though these rulers were worshipped almost as gods, they were often powerless against ambitious nobles. Because there was no clear way to choose a new ruler when an emperor or empress died, civil war often broke out between rival clans, causing suffering for the whole nation. In 593, the clan nobles were able to agree upon a new empress who belonged to the most powerful clan. However, the real power was to lie with her nephew, Prince Taishi Shotoku, who was married to a woman from another influential clan.

When Prince Shotoku became Regent of Japan, he was only nineteen years old. This remarkable young man was not interested in power for its own sake. He wanted to help his country. This meant keeping the rival clans at peace with each other while he enabled Japan to prosper.

Prince Shotoku knew that Japan's political institutions were not advanced, but far over the sea lay China, her great neighbour. China had influenced Japan in the past, so Prince Shotoku turned there again for inspiration. First he reformed and centralised his government. He based his reforms on the teachings of the Chinese sage, Confucius. Confucius taught that everyone must be responsible for each other's welfare. He said able people should run governments, even if they were commoners, and not just people who inherited power, as was the case in Japan. Inspired by these ideals, Prince Shotoku persuaded the ambitious nobles to give up some of their powers to capable commoners, a policy which improved Japanese government. The prince also adopted the Chinese calendar for Japan, and introduced that country's writing system.

Then the prince sent out messengers across five hundred miles of stormy seas to study Chinese culture. They brought back many artists, artisans and scholars. From them Japanese artists and craftsmen learned new skills that they adapted to form a brilliant new culture. Prince Shotoku did still more for his people. He built highways and irrigation systems. He started social programmes. He erected temples and established a new court near the city of Nara. These buildings are among the oldest surviving wooden buildings on earth. The prince also wrote a history of Japan.

Prince Shotoku also helped to spread a new religion, Buddhism. Until this time, the

Japanese religion, called Shinto, was based on rituals that showed love and respect for nature. Buddhism taught people a way of life based on caring for each other, as well. Buddhism did not replace Shinto – people practised both religions, as they still do today – but it did deeply affect the way people lived. Buddhist values of compassion reduced the amount of violence in Japanese society.

Sometimes people don't like change, but Prince Shotoku's people welcomed the many advances he made. During his reign, Japan became more peaceful and prosperous. Its contact with the Chinese enriched and stimulated its culture. The changes Prince Shotoku brought to Japan have affected its history to this day. Even now, the Japanese honour him as a great Buddhist saint and patron of his country.

Japan evolved its own traditions, like kyudo, a form of archery based upon meditation.

A NEW CULTURE

Although Japan borrowed many ideas from China, its people soon adapted them to their own ways. During Prince Shotoku's reign, new forms of architecture, music, sculpture, painting, textile design and dance developed. Some still flourish in their ancient form, such as *gagaku*, a type of Japanese dance. But the Japanese also created their own unique art forms, such as woodblock prints, paper and fabrics, which are now world famous. Children around the world love *origami*, the Japanese art of paper-folding.

Japanese Buddhists developed art forms like the tea ceremony, flower arranging and archery. Each of these combines a simple activity with strict discipline to create an experience of simplicity and calm.

Eventually, the Japanese integrated Chinese writing symbols, or *kangi*, with their own traditional script, *hiragana*. They loved calligraphy, and wrote masterful poetry and novels. One form of poetry, the *haiku*, has only seventeen syllables. A good haiku makes its readers see, hear and feel as the poet does. It is a form that has inspired poets around the world.

Many of the arts that flowered during the reign of Prince Shotoku are still practised in Japan today. The imperial family of Japan is still descended from Prince Shotoku and the early 'divine' rulers, making it the longest unbroken line of rulers in the world.

PRINCE AND SAINT

We know little about what Prince Shotoku was like as a person. He became regent because he and his wife were related to the most important rival clans. But were there other reasons for choosing him? I think he was also chosen because other people admired him. His actions still tell us that he was courageous, kind and diplomatic. He cared for everyone in his country and gave them a vision to follow.

Prince Shotoku brought peace and prosperity to all levels of society by borrowing ideas from Chinese culture.

When Prince Shotoku sent his messengers to China, students, artisans, merchants and scholars went too. In those days, a voyage of five hundred miles and back was as dangerous as going to the moon would be today. Finding the route must have been difficult, because the pilots had no compass to guide them. If they came too close to land on the way, pirates lay in wait for them. On the open sea they had to brave terrible storms. Many ships were lost. Yet they must have felt that they were sharing not only an adventure but a mission to create a better Japan. The prince gave them that sense of mission.

Through his reforms and encouragement, Prince Shotoku changed the way people thought as well as how they lived. During his lifetime he persuaded the wealthy, ambitious nobles to stop fighting each other, while he bettered the lives of ordinary people. And when he adopted Buddhism, he gave the Japanese a way to care for each other as well as for their beautiful world. They all seem to have loved him.

After Prince Shotoku's death in 622, the great clans again fought for power. The prince's own sons were murdered in the conflict. But his reforms survived the strife. Within a few years, new leaders made sure that they took hold. The prince himself was immortalised as the father of Japanese culture.

Some people change the world through force and fear, but not Prince Shotoku. The Japanese people called him a saint not only because of the good things he did for Japan, but because he was a man of great heart.

JAPAN AND CHINA AROUND THE 4TH–7TH CENTURIES AD

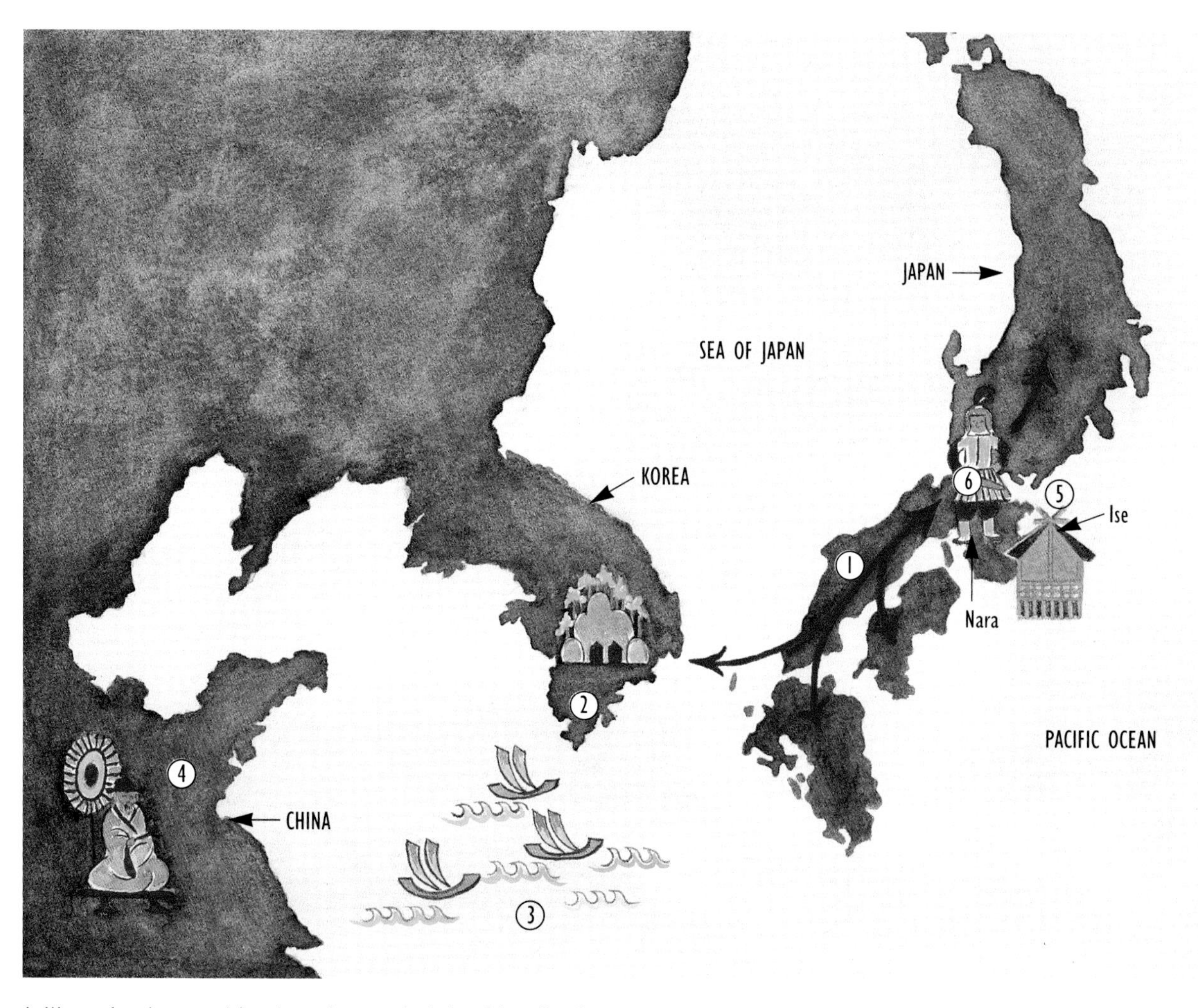

1. Waves of settlers spread into Japan for centuries before Prince Shotoku came to power, many coming through Korea.
2. After the early clans had colonised Japan, they spread back to the mainland, conquering part of southern Korea.
3. Prince Shotoku's fleet of ships avoided Korea, where it no longer had a foothold, and made a longer and more dangerous journey to China.
4. China's emperor thought it only natural that Japan would want to copy his country, but the Japanese used Chinese ideas in their own way.
5. The early Japanese rulers claimed descent from the sun goddess Amaterasu. Her main shrine, still the most important in Japan, is at Ise.
6. Prince Shotoku established his court near Nara, in central Japan.

Mansa Kankan Musa

In 1324, a great Muslim emperor arrived in Egypt. Mansa Musa (or 'Emperor Moses') was on pilgrimage from Mali in West Africa to the holy city of Mecca in Arabia. His journey took about a year, for his empire was thousands of miles away. About eighty thousand people came with him, including slaves, servants, warriors and wives. They rode camels or horses, or walked in ranks carrying solid gold batons.

Mansa Musa brought with him some 150 tons of gold as spending money. He visited Cairo, where he spent and gave away so much gold that its value dropped for years. He was so devout that he preferred visiting mosques to paying his respects to the Sultan of Egypt and had to be persuaded to call on him before he gave offence. Everywhere they went, he and his retinue impressed people with their good manners and generosity.

Through trade, Mansa Musa's gold and his name made their way to Europe. Africa was a mystery to Europeans. They thought it was full of terrifying monsters. The vast Sahara Desert and the unfriendly Islamic countries of North Africa kept them out. Mansa Musa changed their picture of Africa. For centuries afterwards, merchants and adventurers tried to find a direct route to his marvellous wealth.

Mansa Musa became legendary in West Africa for his wisdom as well as his wealth. He ruled the second-largest empire in the world, stretching from the Atlantic Ocean in the west to grasslands in the east, and from the Sahara Desert in the north to jungles in the south. (The Mongol empire of Asia was the largest.) He held absolute power over many different tribes with differing languages, customs and religions.

Mansa Musa made cities like Timbuktu into famous trading centres. Their merchants took gold, ivory, copper, salt and cola nuts away in long caravans. They crossed the Sahara Desert and returned months later with fabrics, horses, swords and knives, books and precious writing paper. Within Mali, craftsmen, weavers, tailors and metalsmiths in the cities traded with artisans, farmers and fishermen from the countryside. Everyone prospered.

As emperor, Mansa Musa could have satisfied his every desire. Instead, he chose to use his resources for the benefit of his people. He made sure all his subjects were safe and well governed. He encouraged them to be creative and to respect one another.

With so much power, Mansa Musa could have been greedy or cruel, like so many rulers have been. But this great king wanted the best for his subjects. Instead of provoking fear,

as previous rulers had done, he inspired love and respect. Long after his death, people remembered him as the ruler who put his subjects first.

FABULOUS KINGDOMS

African gold stirred the curiosity and greed of European adventurers. Looking for its famous wealth, they explored Africa's coastline but found few paths into its heartland. Later, Europeans and North and South Americans created wealth for themselves – by selling African slaves in Europe and then the Americas. They learned little about Africa itself, treated their captives worse than they did animals, and created a picture in their minds of an inferior black race with no history and no culture.

Nothing could have been more untrue. Africa had its own history, as full of glamour and drama as anywhere on earth. Mansa Musa's fabulous empire was part of that history. It was the second of three great empires – Ghana, Mali and Songhai – that arose in western Africa,

Even the great cities have faded away, though Timbuktu still has the same architecture that was introduced by Mansa Musa's architects.

south of the Sahara Desert. Mali was founded in the thirteenth century by the great 'Hungering Lion', Sundiata, when he defeated the oppressive ruler of the last remnant of Ghana. Sundiata became one of West Africa's greatest heroes, because he brought not only victory but well-being to his subjects.

Almost nothing of Mansa Musa's empire has survived. A few statues shaped like this figure have been found in the remains of the city of Djenne.

Mansa Musa was Sundiata's descendant. The Mali empire was in trouble by that time. Some of the emperors after Sundiata had been weak and greedy, and one had been viciously insane. Mansa Musa took charge of his people. He used diplomacy where he could, and war where he needed it, to gain control over most of West Africa. He established a government that did not get bogged down in tribal conflicts that could tear an empire apart. His officials were honest and had to answer to him. He made sure that people could travel safely anywhere in Mali and be met with hospitality.

When Mansa Musa returned from Mecca, he brought back advisers, scholars and even a famous architect who created a new kind of architecture for the emperor's building projects. He constructed mosques and public buildings in his cities, and founded a university in Timbuktu. As learning spread throughout the empire, Mali became famous throughout the Muslim world as an important centre of learning and wisdom. In contrast, Europeans were facing the twin disasters of plague and war.

Mansa Musa might have witnessed traditional tribal dances when headdresses like this were used, just as they are today.

THE SACRED EMPEROR

We are still learning about life in the empire of Mansa Musa, but there is no doubt that he was the centre of its existence. He was evidently not only a competent ruler and general, but he was also known as a joyous and generous person. When his armies conquered new lands, he did not depose the former kings. Instead, he allowed them to stay in power under him. To make sure they stayed loyal and just, he took their sons home as hostages. Then he raised them as his own and even made some of them into generals. He aimed to bring out the best in those around him.

Mansa Musa's main concern was that all his subjects be treated fairly. He was both the lawmaker and the supreme court, and anyone had the right to appeal to him for justice. At the same time, he was not someone you could just approach casually. The emperor was sacred to his people. He was surrounded by splendour. Royal musicians announced his entry. The best horses and warriors were on hand to await his commands. When he held court, he sat under a huge silk umbrella, carried by one of his Turkish slaves. On either side of him stood two huge elephant tusks. His solid-gold bow, arrows, sword and spear rested nearby. As the highest-ranking man in the land, he wore voluminous silk trousers. Beside him stood the royal executioner, ready to mete out justice on the spot.

When his subjects approached him, they knelt down and sprinkled dust on their heads as a mark of respect. Then they could speak their business. Mansa Musa rarely spoke with his subjects directly. His orders always went through his spokesman.

In fact, he was so sacred that no one was even allowed to see him eat. His senior wife brought him food, and then left. Then this mighty emperor, seated on elegant cushions and carpets, surrounded by silk hangings, could begin his meal, all alone.

MANSA MUSA'S AFRICA

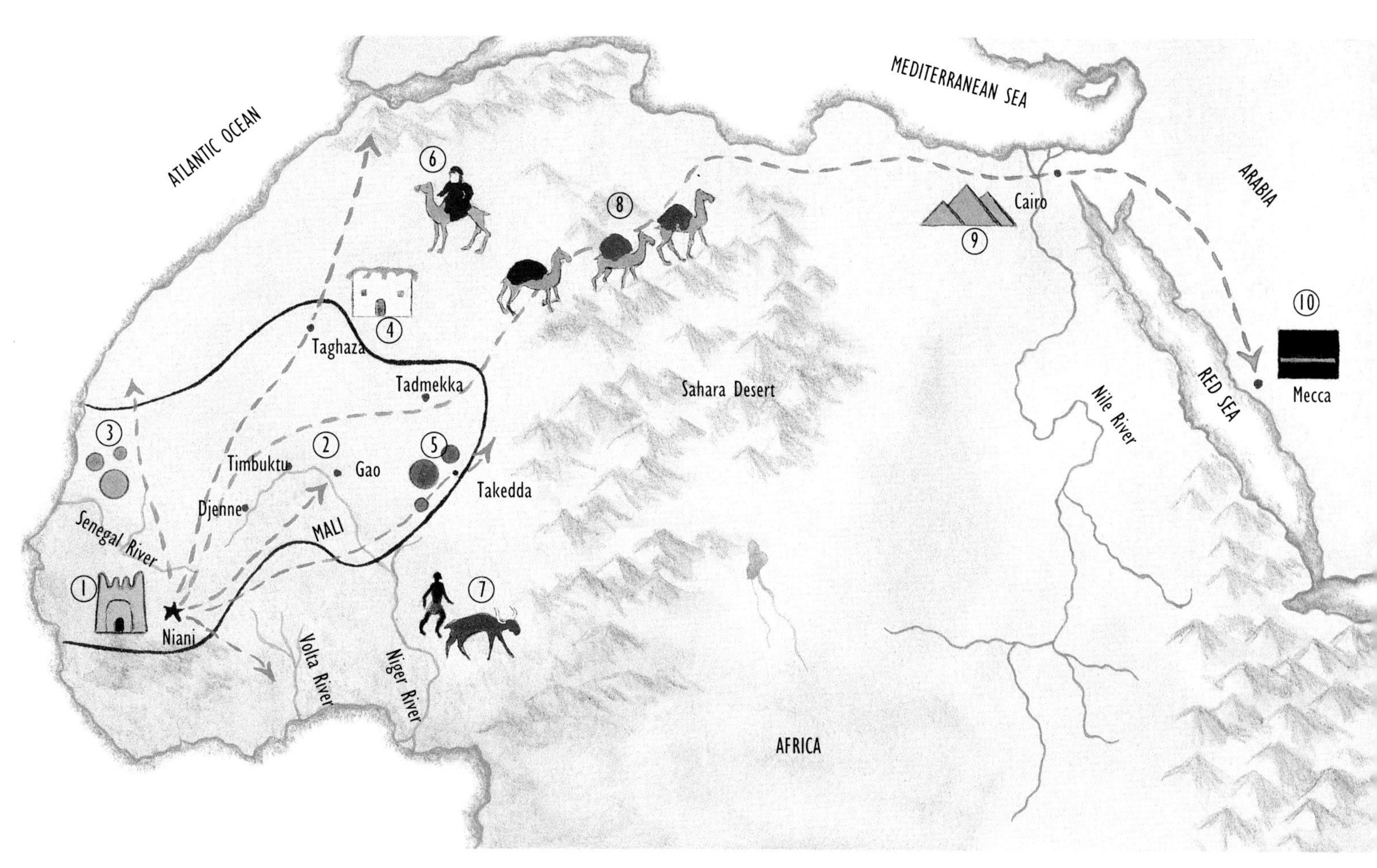

1. Mansa Musa's capital was at Niani. Little remains of it now.
2. Major trading cities like Djenne, Timbuktu, Gao and Tadmekka linked Mali with the rest of Africa.
3. Gold was mined in this area, but the location of the gold mines was always kept secret. Today most of the gold is gone.
4. Mali's wealth depended on salt as much as gold. This was mined in the desert, in Taghaza, a city where even the houses were built of blocks of salt.
5. Another source of wealth was copper, mined at Takedda.
6. Nomadic Tuareg tribesmen led most of the caravans across the Sahara Desert. They gave allegiance to the empire of Mali.
7. Other tribes within the empire herded cattle, farmed, or specialised in crafts such as weaving or pottery.
8. Mansa Musa's long pilgrimage to Mecca was difficult and dangerous, yet thousands of people joined him.
9. Once the centre of a great Egyptian empire, Cairo was now part of the Islamic world. Mansa Musa would have passed the Pyramids, already ancient in his time.
10. In Mecca, Mansa Musa would have visited the Kaaba, the holiest shrine in the Muslim world.

Leonardo da Vinci

Leonardo da Vinci was possibly the greatest genius in history. An artist, scientist, engineer, architect, inventor and musician, he came to symbolise his era – that of the Italian Renaissance. Though he was courted by princes and kings, few people fully appreciated the true breadth of his genius, because his ideas were centuries ahead of their time.

Leonardo was born in 1452 in Vinci, Italy. Early on, his family realised how bright, curious and talented he was. Even as a child, he could already use both left and right hands with equal ease. His parents apprenticed him to Verrocchio, a leading artist in nearby Florence, one of the artistic centres of Italy. In those days, artists were regarded as craftsmen and apprentices worked together in studios under a master artist. Leonardo learned painting, sculpture, music, mathematics and science from Verrocchio and, with other students, worked on projects ranging from painting to sculpture and architecture. By the time Leonardo was grown up, he was already a famous artist and musician, ready to explore the world.

Florence was one of five great Italian city-states. When Leonardo was a young man, he moved to Milan, another powerful city-state. His patron (employer) was the city's ruler, Ludovico Sforza. Leonardo worked in Milan for many years, not only as an artist and musician but as an engineer, inventor and producer of pageants and parades. His paintings completely revolutionised the world of art. Up until then, art mostly had been used to illustrate religious themes. It was often stylised and lifeless, sometimes reduced to mere decoration. Leonardo's paintings revealed a realistic world full of mystery and meaning. Artists from all over Europe came to Milan to study them.

Many people regard Leonardo as the first true scientist, because he observed his world in such detail and with such an open mind, and because he explained why things happened. He was fascinated by everything, and to him there was no separation between art and science. He filled many notebooks with his ideas, making drawings and writing down his observations about nature. He studied plants, animals, anatomy and the flight of birds; he observed the patterns of water and wind, light and shadow, and the movement of heavenly bodies. On paper he 'invented' aeroplanes, war tanks, paddle-boats, and many other things that are only now in use. To keep his notes to himself, he wrote backwards. To read them, anyone else had to hold up his notes in front of a mirror!

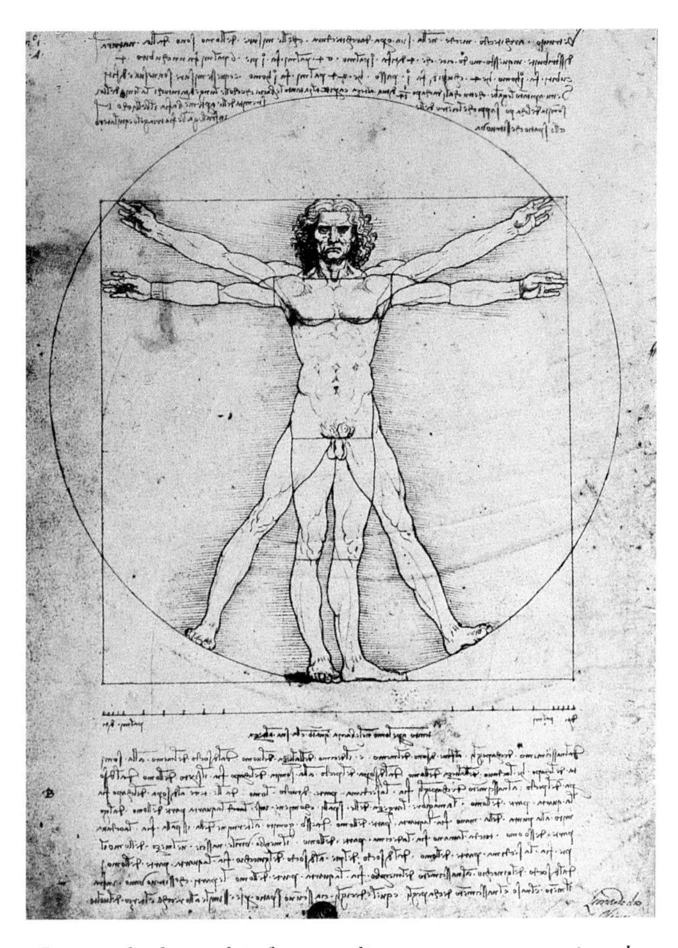

Leonardo drew this famous diagram – representing the proportions of the human body mathematically – for a friend's book.

However, Leonardo never completed some of his projects, and others began to fall apart soon after they were finished. Leonardo's famous wall painting *The Last Supper* started to disintegrate almost at once because he had tried a new paint formula. His curiosity often led him from one idea or invention to another. He always meant to come back and finish a project, but often another good idea would pop up and he would begin work on that instead. In other cases, his work was interrupted by the outbreak of war.

In 1499, Milan was invaded by France. Leonardo left and spent several years working in one Italian city-state after another. He travelled to Mantua, where a noblewoman, Isabella d'Este, asked him to paint her portrait. He never did, but her numerous letters to him tell us many things about him that we wouldn't have known otherwise.

He then travelled to Venice. The city was at war with the Turks and its leaders asked Leonardo how they might defend it. He suggested that the Venetians should flood the area around their city if the Turks attacked it. Luckily, the Turks never attacked.

Leonardo added to his discoveries wherever he went, while all around him countries and cities fought and destroyed each other. One commission Leonardo received was to inspect fortifications for one of Italy's most ruthless tyrants, Cesare Borgia. Borgia was so bloodthirsty that Leonardo finally left the job. Fortunately, Borgia ignored Leonardo's ideas for making better weapons, such as cannon that could fire exploding cannonballs.

Leonardo was never able to settle down and concentrate on anything for very long, and the continual wars made no sense to him. While he was frequently commissioned to design weapons and defence systems – work that he enjoyed as he could never resist exploring his own ideas – Leonardo found war itself 'a bestial madness'. He foresaw that the 'arms race' of his own time could only cause increasing trouble for humankind. In one of his notebooks he wrote: 'Ambitious people, never content with the world's gifts of life and beauty, ruin their own lives and can never benefit from the utility and beauty of the world.'

Getting on in years and growing tired, Leonardo even tried working for the Pope in Rome, where all the best artists were flocking. Younger rivals were being given work that would previously have been offered to him. Thus it was not him but Michelangelo who received a commission to design the huge dome for the great basilica of St Peter, and to paint the Sistine Chapel. Leonardo was treated as a has-been.

As an old man, Leonardo moved to France to work for King Francis I. He spent his last years there, working on his ideas and entertaining the king. His notes filled thousands of pages. He had hoped they would be published after his death to benefit humanity. Instead, they were hidden in collections across Europe, where people had no access to them for three hundred years. By then, many of his observations had been made by others. Had they been available sooner, the entire history of Western science may have been quite different.

Many of Leonardo's paintings were also lost, but today we can see in museums around the world those that have survived – not to mention the Internet, where one of the most popular 'sites' is the Leonardo da Vinci Virtual Museum. And today we can see some of his ideas brought to life, from helicopters and diving suits to a frogman's flippers.

THE RENAISSANCE

Leonardo was born into exciting times. All across Europe, people were dropping old ways of thinking and doing. For centuries, the Church had taught them that life was full of sin, death and judgement. Now they

Although he released them out of compassion, Leonardo also studied birds carefully, observing aspects of their flight that were not confirmed until the invention of the slow-motion camera.

began to celebrate life, and to value their human qualities. Ancient Greek science and philosophy came to light, with their emphasis on rational thought. Through the study of mathematics and philosophy, geography and astronomy, people began examining the world around them and what lay beyond it. Printed books spread ideas everywhere. Explorers seeking wealth crossed land and sea. With so many new discoveries, people named their times the Renaissance, or time of rebirth.

However, these times were also difficult. In Europe countries and cities were at war. In Italy, city-states were often ruled by tyrannical and devious men. Republican Florence was lucky to have fairly decent leaders, however. Proud of their city, artists like Leonardo made it beautiful. But Florence also had to play power politics with other city-states. Leonardo probably went to Milan as a way of improving relations between the two cities.

After leaving Milan, Leonardo received many commissions around Italy. One of them was for the portrait called the *Mona Lisa*, now the most famous painting in history. His work varied from painting portraits and battle scenes to designing cannon, and drainage and canal systems. But Leonardo did not wait for a commission to have ideas. For instance, because he believed that plague struck when people lived too close together (partially true), he designed the first spacious 'suburbs'. He tried to persuade the Sultan of Turkey to hire him to build the longest and highest bridge in the world. He applied mathematical principles to everything: from music and art, to human proportions and the flight of cannonballs. He drew beautiful and accurate maps. Wherever he went, Leonardo was welcomed as the ideal Renaissance man, because he was good at so many different things.

LONELY GENIUS

Leonardo loved animals and hated cruelty towards them. He even became a vegetarian. He sometimes bought caged birds just to set them free. He especially loved horses, and drew beautiful sketches of them. In fact, one of his greatest disappointments was a failed project when he was in Milan to cast the statue of a horse that would have been 24 feet high. He had made a spectacular life-size clay model for it, which was on public display. But the bronze he was to use for it was shipped away to make cannon for battle. Then, after Milan was invaded by France, soldiers used the model for target practice. After a while, it fell apart.

Although he remained generous as a teacher, inventor and idea-maker to the end of his days, it seems that he grew ever lonelier. Perhaps he felt disappointed with his fellow men, whose appetite for war never ended, whose imaginations could never match his own, and who could never seem to appreciate the wonderful world in quite the same way he did.

LEONARDO'S ITALY

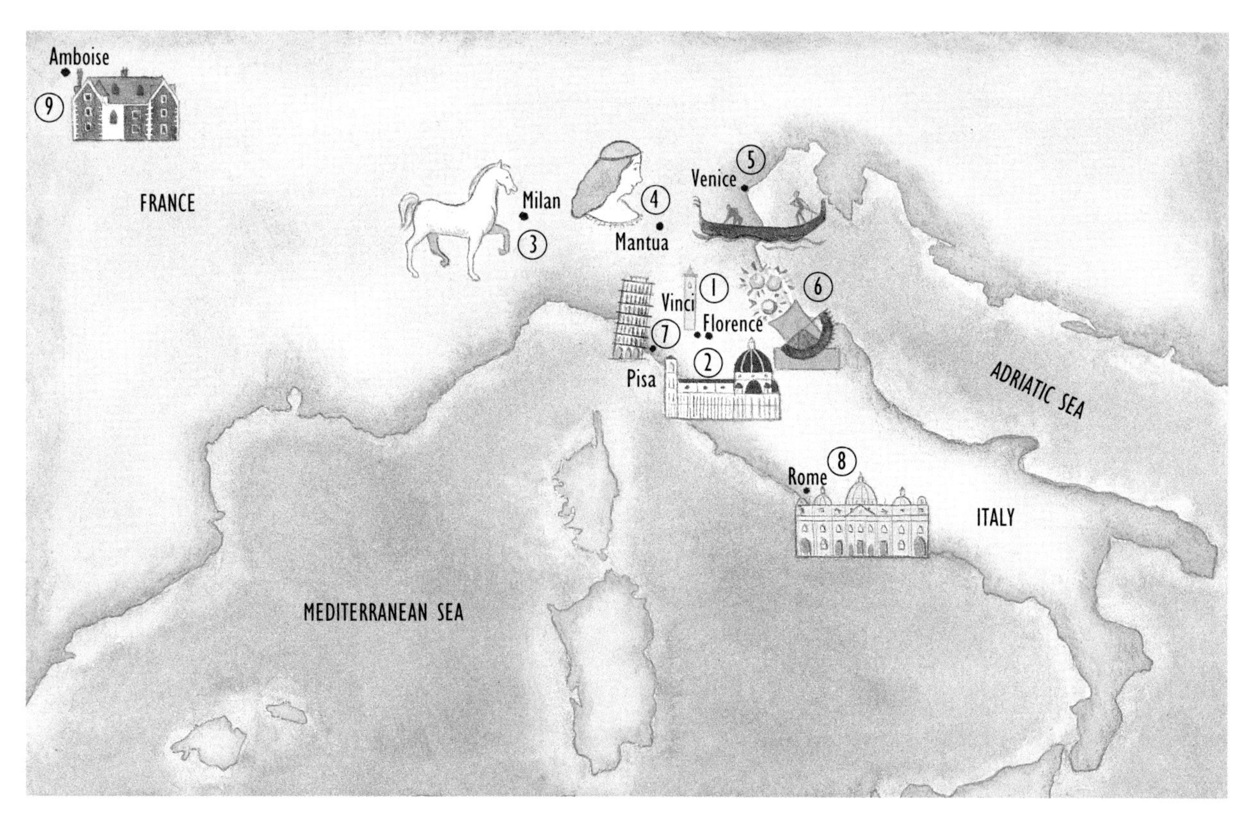

1. Leonardo was born in the tiny village of Vinci, west of Florence, and was baptised under this church tower.

2. Leonardo was apprenticed to the artist Verrocchio in Florence. He may have helped Verrocchio design a golden ball to be placed on top of the huge dome of the Cathedral of Santa Maria del Fiore.

3. In his early twenties, Leonardo set off for Milan. There he painted *The Last Supper* and began the great horse sculpture that was never cast.

4. After France invaded Milan, Leonardo visited Mantua briefly, where Isabella d'Este demanded that he paint her portrait.

5. Leonardo visited Venice, where its leaders asked him how to defend their city.

6. Now courted by many patrons, Leonardo spent several years in and around Florence again. One patron was the warlike tyrant Cesare Borgia.

7. Leonardo was also asked to help Florence in its siege of Pisa, whose famous tower did not lean so much as it does today.

8. Leonardo even tried working for the Pope in Rome, but he was considered too old.

9. Leonardo crossed the Alps to be the guest of the King of France at Amboise. Here Leonardo was respected and well cared for, and it was here that he eventually died.

William Shakespeare

About four hundred years ago, when William Shakespeare began writing and performing plays for his fellow Englishmen, he didn't realise he would become the greatest playwright in history. He just wanted to entertain people.

Shakespeare was born in Stratford-upon-Avon in 1564. Young Will received a good basic education, but he also learned from the world around him. He had an eye for detail, an ear for the rhythms of speech and a quick mind. As a young man, he left his wife and children at home and set off for London to try his fortune in the theatre.

Plays were increasingly popular in those days. Early miracle and morality plays devised for religious festivals had given way to performances full of action, violence and romance. Actors and playwrights were in great demand. Shakespeare showed he could not only act but write, and he became one of London's favourites.

At one point, plague broke out in London. Theatres had to shut down to prevent its spread, and acting troupes fled to the countryside. There they toured about, spreading the popularity of Shakespeare's plays.

During this time, Shakespeare turned his hand to poetry, creating some of the most beautiful and mysterious poems in our language. He cleverly dedicated some of them to a wealthy noble, who rewarded him generously. When the plague died down, Shakespeare used this money to buy into part ownership of a theatre just outside London. He now received income as an actor, as an author and as a theatre owner.

Shakespeare's actors called themselves the Lord Chamberlain's Men, using the title of the powerful noble who became their patron. His plays were even performed for Queen Elizabeth I. Shakespeare probably acted in some of them. After the queen's death, the new ruler, King James I, liked Shakespeare's plays and acting company so well that he became their patron and they became the King's Men.

Shakespeare eventually grew wealthy and he retired, returning to his family in Stratford. He wrote a few more plays, but he enjoyed life in the country too much to return to London. He died surrounded by loving family and friends.

However, his plays were nearly lost. He never published them for fear they would fall into a rival troupe's hands. Without the devotion of his friends, Shakespeare's work might have been forgotten. They realised he had written plays of true genius. After his death, two good

friends from his troupe reconstructed them from memory, notes and some inferior pirated versions used by rival companies. They put them together in a collection and had them published. In the introduction, his famous friend Ben Jonson said prophetically: 'He was not for an age but for all time.'

ALL THE WORLD'S A STAGE

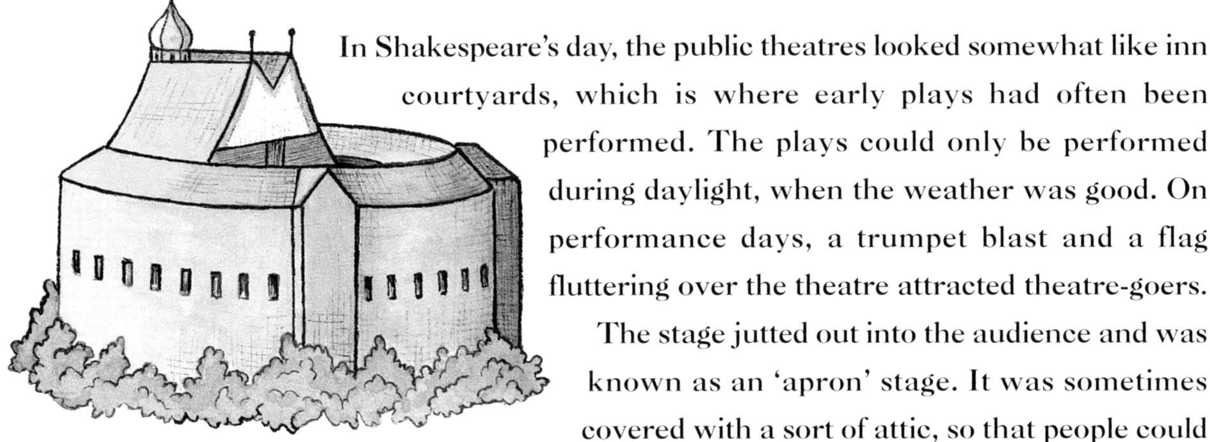

Did Shakespeare's Globe Theatre look like this?

In Shakespeare's day, the public theatres looked somewhat like inn courtyards, which is where early plays had often been performed. The plays could only be performed during daylight, when the weather was good. On performance days, a trumpet blast and a flag fluttering over the theatre attracted theatre-goers.

The stage jutted out into the audience and was known as an 'apron' stage. It was sometimes covered with a sort of attic, so that people could be let down by ropes if the script called for a god to descend from above. A trap door on the stage floor allowed actors to rise from underneath, too. The attic was nicknamed Heaven and the area beneath the stage was Hell. There were no realistic sets. One bush might represent a forest, or someone might carry a sign on stage stating where a scene was taking place.

Wealthy spectators sat in tiers of booths all around the stage while common folk stood on the ground under the open sky. Although they interrupted the action, show-offs could sometimes pay extra to sit on the stage itself. People expected to be entertained, and they threw garbage at the performers if they weren't!

... Or like this? The only two pictures of it disagree.

All the actors were men, or young boys with high voices and no beards. The boys played the female roles, because acting was considered too coarse a profession for women. The actors wore rich costumes that once had belonged to the nobility. These costumes rarely matched the play's setting. Instead, for a play set in ancient Greece, one actor might wear a piece of armour that looked vaguely antique. The audience had to supply other details from their own imaginations.

Because sets and costumes were not realistic, props and sound effects were all important. For instance, during fight scenes an actor carried a pig's bladder filled with blood under his clothes. When he was 'stabbed', he could bleed realistically. The audience loved it! For the sound of thunder, someone rolled cannonballs around in 'Heaven'. Cannon were fired during battle scenes, too. In fact, during one play, the shot from the cannon set Shakespeare's theatre on fire and burned it to the ground!

Shakespeare's plays were perfect for the audiences and theatres of his time. Knowing that plays were equally popular with nobles, the wealthy and ordinary folk, he learned how to appeal to them all. With only costumes and props, and no breaks for scene changes, the action and dialogue had to stir people's imaginations. Shakespeare's plays were filled with rich images from nature and daily life that allowed people to imagine the action better.

Not all performances were held at the Globe. Shakespeare's troupe performed for royalty and the nobility in their great halls.

During Shakespeare's lifetime, England was enjoying the Elizabethan Renaissance – so named after Queen Elizabeth I. She herself was especially fond of plays. Shakespeare happily slipped in references to events and places that reflected English history and achievements. He also used stories familiar to everyone, including Greek myths and Roman history.

Shakespeare used the English language playfully, inventing puns and figures of speech that we still use today. Here are a few: 'tongue-tied', 'high time', 'seen better days' and 'dead as a doornail'. He invented words like hurry, lonely, excellent and leapfrog, and almost two thousand others that we still use every day. In doing so he helped create a vigorous national language that reflected England's rising status in the world.

Shakespeare knew that even serious dramas had to have a little humour in them. Other playwrights added slapstick and clowning around to make people laugh, but not to make their plays better. His tragedies had humour in them, but they were relevant to the plot. In the same way, his comedies often had something thought-provoking to say.

Finally, Shakespeare wrote with such insight into how people feel and behave that his characters seemed totally believable. He put the world on to his stage and made people laugh, cry or think deeply. He still does. Because his plays were about the human qualities we all share, they transcended their times, and still capture people's imaginations.

THE IMMORTAL BARD

Shakespeare became the most popular dramatist in history; today his plays are performed in more languages and in more countries than those of any other playwright. They have been translated into almost a hundred different languages. So much has been written about him and his works that the Folger Shakespeare Library in Washington, DC, is crammed with thousands of books. His plays have inspired ballets, operas, musicals and movies. Children study them at school, often unwillingly because Shakespeare's language is antiquated and is sometimes hard to understand at first. And he would have understood. He wrote about unwilling schoolboys, and had been one himself. But school was much harsher in his day, with long hours and frequent whippings for misbehaviour.

The Globe Theatre was recently reconstructed in London on the banks of the Thames and today Shakespeare's plays can be watched in a similar setting to the one in which they were first performed. But at least modern audiences, who watch the plays in the open air like the commoners did in Shakespeare's time, can use a new-fangled invention – the umbrella – to keep themselves dry!

Shakespeare would also be amused to know that a special word was invented to describe people's admiration for him: 'bardolatry'. It combines the word 'bard', or storyteller, with the word 'idolatry'. Some people have reacted against idolising Shakespeare, even asserting that, as a commoner with a limited education, he could not have written such great plays. They have tried to claim that someone noble, or even royal, like Queen Elizabeth I, must have written them. But serious historians laugh at these claims, because Shakespeare's life and fame are well documented.

While the language of Shakespeare may seem difficult to understand on the page, when performed his plays blossom into life. Though our language has changed so much since his time, Shakespeare's understanding of human nature, his humour and his way with words ensure that he will remain the Immortal Bard.

SHAKESPEARE'S ENGLAND

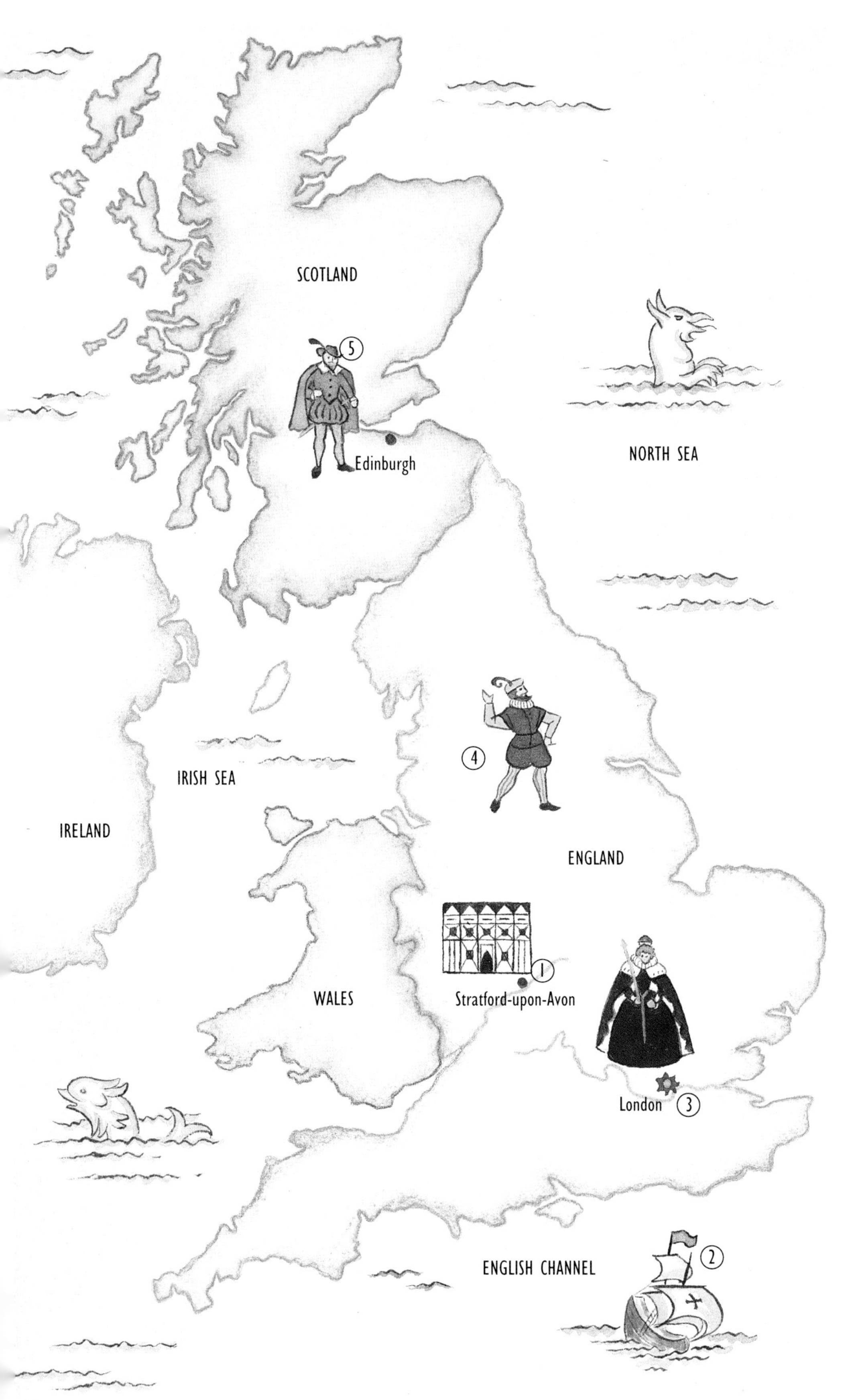

1. Shakespeare was born, raised and married in Stratford-upon-Avon, eventually retiring there. He probably visited his family here only once a year while he lived in London.
2. Shakespeare was a boy when the English navy defeated the invading Spanish Armada. Such achievements probably contributed to his sense of England's destiny.
3. It was in London that Shakespeare grew to fame as an actor, playwright and poet. Queen Elizabeth I was one of his fans.
4. In 1593, when plague struck London, Shakespeare's actors toured the countryside.
5. Another great fan of Shakespeare was James I, King of England and Scotland, who succeeded Queen Elizabeth.

Benjamin Franklin

You probably know that Benjamin Franklin was a 'Founding Father' of the United States, but did you know he was also a printer, author, public servant, inventor, scientist and ambassador? His energy, wit and optimism helped shape the new nation and the way its people saw themselves. His inventions and scientific discoveries made him just as well loved in Europe.

Ben Franklin was born in Boston, Massachusetts, in 1706. With seventeen children, his parents could only afford to send him to school for two years. Then they apprenticed him to an older brother who ran a printing business. Ben continued his education through books, which were scarce in those days. Socrates was his hero.

Ben's brother treated him so harshly that he ran away at the age of seventeen. In the next few years he prospered, though. After working in England, he moved to Philadelphia, Pennsylvania, founded his own printing business and newspaper, married and started a family.

Ben began publishing an almanac, which he called *Poor Richard's Almanack*, filled with astronomical tables, astrology, recipes, jokes and proverbs like 'The early bird gets the worm'. The *Almanack* made him famous throughout the American colonies. Only the Bible was more widely read.

Ben Franklin believed that ordinary people working together could create the same benefits for themselves that were enjoyed by the nobility and the wealthy. He helped establish the first public library in North America, a police force, volunteer fire department, a hospital and an academy that became the University of Pennsylvania. Roads were merely dirt tracks then, but as postmaster of the colonies he made the postal service fast and reliable, giving the colonies a greater sense of community. He even organised the first 'garbage service'!

All his life, Franklin looked to improve things. He invented a fireplace insert that gave out more heat and is still used today, along with lightning rods, bifocal glasses, the gliding rocking chair, and more. He even invented a musical instrument using glass bells called the armonica. He never patented his inventions; they were for everyone. People all over the colonies and Europe were especially grateful for the stove and lightning rod, which made their homes warmer and safer.

Franklin was a shrewd but honest businessman, proud of his humble origins. When he was forty-two, an advanced age in those days, he retired and pursued his own interests. He

learned French, Spanish, Italian, German and Latin; worked for the colonial government; continued to invent things; and became interested in electricity.

At that time the science of electricity was a mystery, with no practical applications. Franklin devised various experiments to find out about it. In one, he proved that lightning was electricity by flying a kite in a lightning storm and drawing off an electric charge. Luckily, he wasn't killed! He invented words to describe his findings, like battery, conductor, and plus and minus charges. His experiments made him famous as a scientist.

Always active in politics, Ben Franklin was sent to England to represent the colonies. While crossing the Atlantic, he observed the Gulf Stream, a current which circulates around the ocean and can leave sailing ships becalmed. He prompted the ship's captain to chart its movements, to help navigators.

In England, he spent many frustrating years lobbying lawmakers to persuade them to uphold colonial rights. Meanwhile, he made friends all over Europe, continued inventing and experimenting, and began an autobiography that is still fun to read.

In 1775, realising that England was never going to listen to the colonies' grievances, he returned home to support the American Revolution. He helped draft the Declaration of Independence, and then sailed to France, England's old enemy, where he urged the French to help the revolutionaries. At the end of the Revolution, he negotiated peace with England and became the first US ambassador to France.

Home at last and failing in health, Franklin helped draft the new US Constitution. After his death, France actually held a larger funeral for him than the Americans did. This man of many talents had belonged not only to the USA but to the world.

Settlers poured into North America from Europe looking for a new start in life. They saw the land as a vast wilderness waiting to be tamed by hard work.

THE 'NEW WORLD'

The American colonies offered opportunities for thousands of people. Displacing the Native Americans, English, Scots, Irish,

Welsh and even Dutch and Germans poured into the colonies. Some were looking for religious freedom not found in Europe. Some wanted land. Others were merchants who imported what the colonists wanted, such as tea and cloth – and African slaves – and exported animal pelts, salted fish, and tobacco.

Franklin enjoyed playing the plain-spoken rustic for the adoring French aristocracy.

Villages along the Atlantic coast grew into cities. Their streets were alternately muddy and dusty. Houses crowded together burned down before anyone could help. With insanitary living conditions and little medical knowledge, smallpox hit repeatedly. Inland, settlers built trading posts, farms and forts. They confronted the elements, huge forests, wide rivers, disease and hostile natives. They learned to make what they needed, from homespun clothing to horseshoes, or to do without. But always there was the promise of a prosperity denied them in Europe.

As they put down roots, the colonists realised they could produce and export their own goods. But English trading companies, protected by law, monopolised colonial trade. The British government profited from this system through taxes on trade goods. There seemed to be more taxes all the time. In the 1760s, England had defeated France after a long war, winning Canada. It expected the colonies to pay for the victory.

When an English law or tax seemed unjust, colonials had difficulty getting Parliament to listen to their grievances. For example, wealthy nobles owned the colony of Pennsylvania. These 'proprietors' lived luxuriously in England, indifferent to the hard life in America. The colonial governors worked for them. When taxes were raised for a militia to protect against Native American raiders, the nobles were exempted, even though they benefited. Those same nobles participated in Parliament and lobbied against the colonists, who had no representatives.

Such conflicts came to boiling point in the late 1700s. When Ben Franklin went to England, he assumed colonists had the same rights all Englishmen had. He was confident Parliament would listen, but was met with hostility, arrogance and indifference. But he still loved England and was loyal to the end. Only when members of Parliament launched a vicious verbal attack on him did he recognise that his loyalty must now be to America, and to the new world he had helped to shape.

SILENCE DOGOOD AND OTHER CHARACTERS

Ben Franklin helped mould the character of the colonies with the 'characters' he created during his life. When apprenticed to his older brother, he wanted to contribute to his brother's newspaper. Knowing he wouldn't take him seriously, Ben invented a character, 'Silence Dogood'. He left 'her' letters at the print shop after work, where his brother found and printed them. Poking fun at Bostonians' prejudices, they also championed ideas like freedom of speech and education for women. They were an instant success.

Years later, Franklin invented another character for *Poor Richard's Almanack*. In it, 'Poor Richard' humorously reported on life with his bossy wife. He was also the mouthpiece for Ben Franklin's ideas about freedom, justice and public spirit. These ideas helped shape his fellow colonials' attitudes and paved the way for a democracy after the American Revolution.

Even later, as an old man, Ben Franklin himself became a 'character' when he arrived in France to promote the American Revolution. He was greeted by adoring crowds. They wanted to see the great scientist who had tamed lightning. Dressed for his journey in simple dark clothing and a beaverskin hat, he became an instant fashion sensation.

Franklin actually liked to dress elegantly, but when he saw the impact his travelling clothes made on the French, he played his new role to the hilt. He continued to dress simply and created an image of the new American, earthy and plain-speaking. Mingling with the French nobility, he enjoyed their hero worship.

Ben Franklin played many roles as he continued to learn from life. As he grew old, he was able to drop many of the prejudices of his time. He came to realise the evils of slavery and the hypocrisy of white savagery towards 'primitive' natives.

Franklin became the model for the self-made man who works hard and honestly to better his own life and the lives of others. At the end of his life he wrote: 'God grant that not only the love of liberty, but a thorough knowledge of the rights of man, may pervade all the nations of the earth, so that a philosopher may set his foot anywhere on its surface, and say, "This is my country."'

BENJAMIN FRANKLIN'S WORLD

1. Benjamin Franklin was born in Boston and learned the printing business from his brother.

2. Franklin ran away to Philadelphia, returning there after a spell in England. In Philadelphia he eventually became not only a successful printer but also a prominent citizen and scientist.

3. Franklin sailed to England again, this time as an important man. He observed the course of the Gulf Stream and had his captain map it out for him.

4. During the years leading up to the American Revolution, Franklin represented colonial interests in London.

5. Benjamin Franklin also served as the first US ambassador to France.

Wolfgang Amadeus Mozart

Have you ever sung 'Twinkle Twinkle Little Star'? Did you know Wolfgang Amadeus Mozart probably wrote it, when he was only five years old? Mozart was born in Austria in 1756. Both his father Leopold and his older sister Nannerl were talented musicians, but neither of them could match little Wolfgang. By the age of five he had mastered the piano and violin and was writing his own music.

His father decided to profit from his children's talents. Surely rulers and nobles all over Europe would love these musical child prodigies and shower them with money and gifts? Leopold set off with Nannerl and Wolfgang on a series of performing tours across Europe. In those days, fathers had absolute control over their families, and no one thought it odd for Leopold to put his children to work. He was proud of them.

Everywhere they went, the children delighted audiences. They performed for kings, queens, nobles and churchmen, and indeed received gifts: money, clothes, wigs, a little sword for Wolfgang, watches and musical boxes. They had to work long hours, and both fell seriously ill several times. However, they loved seeing the big world, and Wolfgang met other fine musicians who taught him more about music.

In eighteenth-century Europe, musicians and composers were supported by the wealthy ruling classes. As Mozart grew up, he too began to look for wealthy patrons. But despite his talent, he never seemed to find a suitable position. One reason was that jealous rivals intrigued against him behind his back. Another was Mozart's own independent spirit. He wanted respect for himself and his music.

By his mid-twenties, Mozart realised that he would not find a permanent patron. He now had a wife and children to support. He tried making a living by teaching music, giving public performances and accepting commissions. He also composed music in the hope of selling it, and he wrote music for his own pleasure.

No matter how hard he worked and how much money he made, Mozart increasingly fell into debt. He was never good with money. After his childhood illnesses, he wasn't strong, either. His constant work and worry about money took its toll. At the age of thirty-five, he fell mortally ill, possibly from kidney disease. He continued to compose even as he lay dying.

Mozart's widow, Constanze, kept his reputation alive, and her second husband wrote Mozart's first biography. More and more of his music came to light. No other composer has ever produced so many different kinds of music, and few have written as much as he did – almost 650 complete pieces. He even wrote a piece for Ben Franklin's armonica.

Mozart knew he was leaving an enormous gift to the world. Today he is more popular than ever. Some scientists even claim that listening to his music can increase your intelligence!

MOZART'S EUROPE

On their tours, the Mozarts grew accustomed to special treatment, since even kings and queens received them so graciously. Once little Wolfgang jumped into the lap of the Austrian empress and gave her a kiss. Luckily, she was amused. Like most rulers of her day, she held absolute power and could have had him punished severely. After all, he was only a servant.

To entertain noble patrons while he was on tour, sometimes little Wolfgang even performed blindfolded.

Although the Mozarts worked for the wealthy nobility, they never thought of themselves as servants. They had friends from many different social levels. However, some of their rivals wanted only to climb higher up the social scale; they snubbed those below them and backstabbed those around them.

As charming young children, Wolfgang and Nannerl threatened no one in this competitive world. When they grew up, though, they were no longer considered cute and unthreatening. Nannerl stopped travelling and began teaching music at home. Because he was small and young-looking, Wolfgang was able to continue longer, but eventually he had to look for work under a wealthy patron. Even though he was admired universally, sometimes rival musicians tried to sabotage him. His sense of his own worth got in his way, too.

The rich people Mozart had to please didn't like his independent ways. They expected him to entertain humbly or glorify them. Once one of Mozart's employers took him on a trip to another city. Mozart hated eating with the servants and waiting around for hours in case his patron might want a little music. The man also paid Mozart poorly but refused to let him earn extra money by composing for anyone else. Mozart finally left in a rage and vowed to make a living independently.

Mozart's desire to earn a living on his own was revolutionary. He wasn't the only one with different ideas, though. During his lifetime, two major political upheavals would shape a new Europe: the American and French Revolutions. Both uprisings came about because common people felt they were being treated unjustly. People across Europe began to question the enormous power held by monarchs and the nobility. Eventually, the system that Mozart found so suffocating began to break down.

Mozart hinted at how people of the 'lower' classes felt in one of his funniest operas. In *The Marriage of Figaro*, the masters are silly and incompetent, while the servants are the clever, capable people. Operas in his time were like films or television are for us. They entertained and they spread ideas. Mozart was no firebrand ready to overthrow the government, but he did poke fun at the class of people who couldn't appreciate his genius.

Operas like 'The Magic Flute' combined music, spectacle, fantasy and perhaps a secret message. Was the Queen of the Night a veiled caricature of the Empress of Austria, whom he had once kissed and now regarded as a tyrant?

FOR THE LOVE OF MUSIC

Mozart learned to read and write music before he could read words. By the time he was eight, he had composed a symphony. By the time he was twelve, he had written his first opera.

Mozart enjoyed writing music even more than performing it. When Mozart created music in later years, it was finished in his head before he ever wrote it down. He knew exactly where he wanted horns or violins or clarinets. Sometimes he had to add on to the bottom of his music sheets to make room for all the different instruments. He rarely made changes as he wrote, and he could write anywhere or at any time. He wrote while talking with friends, playing billiards, and even holding his wife's hand while she was having a baby! He worked late every night, sometimes finishing music only hours before it was to be performed.

Mozart wrote symphonies, operas, church music, light and serious music. He hoped that everyone would enjoy it. And they did. Even common people hummed his tunes walking down the streets, just like we do today with our favourite songs. However, because there were no copyright or royalty laws, even popular music like Mozart's didn't keep making money for him. Unlike today, he only got paid once when the piece was written, and not each time it was played, so he had to continue composing and looking for commissions.

He had to pay another price for his independence. He was constantly in debt because he had to keep up appearances to attract more business. That meant paying for servants, nice clothes, an attractive apartment and entertainment for wealthy friends. But the Mozarts had to do without other things. Once a friend dropped by and found Mozart and Constanze whirling about in their parlour. He thought they were dancing, but Mozart confided that they had run out of firewood and were trying to keep warm, since they couldn't afford more wood.

As he neared the end of his life, Mozart received a commission from a mysterious visitor who wanted him to write a requiem – music for a funeral. The stranger refused to identify himself. He was actually just an agent for someone who bought other people's music to pass off as his own. But Mozart's health was failing. He became convinced that the requiem would be for his own funeral.

Mozart began to pour out compositions, some of his greatest, as though he were running out of time. Then he fell mortally ill. He struggled desperately to finish the requiem, even dictating it to a friend when he grew too weak to write. He did not live to complete it.

Had he lived, probably Mozart would have eventually become successful. He knew that one day his genius would be recognised. We might feel sad that he died so young, but he faced death with confidence. For him, death was part of life, and his life was happy because he spent it doing what he loved.

MOZART TOURS EUROPE

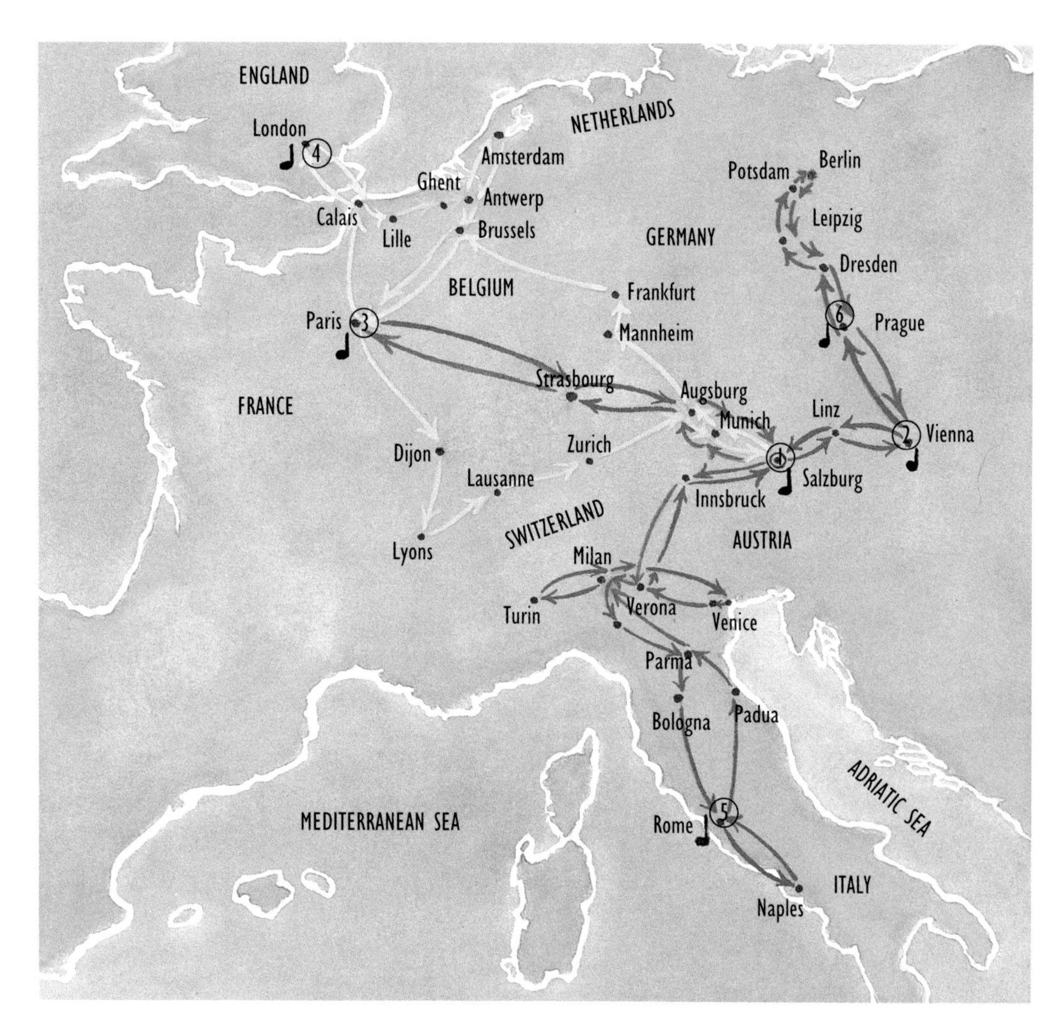

1763–6: MOZART WENT ON HIS FIRST TOUR WITH NANNERL AND THEIR FATHER.

1770: MOZART TOURED AGAIN WITH HIS FATHER; HIS FUTURE SEEMED ASSURED.

1777–8: MOZART TOURED WITH HIS MOTHER.

1789–90: MOZART'S LAST TOUR WAS AN ATTEMPT TO SALVAGE FINANCES.

1. Mozart was born and raised in Salzburg, Austria, but his father took him and his sister all over Europe. Throughout his life, he performed and composed wherever he went.

2. On their first visit to Vienna, the little Mozarts performed for the Empress of Austria. As an adult, Wolfgang and his wife, Constanze, moved to Vienna, where he died in 1791.

3. Mozart made two trips to Paris: on the first, he entertained the king and queen; on the second, he was touring with his mother, trying to find patrons.

4. In London, the Mozarts were welcomed on their first tour. As an adult, Mozart was invited back and, had he lived, he might have found security there.

5. Mozart's second hugely successful tour was to Italy. In Rome, the Pope awarded him the order of the golden spur, a major honour.

6. In Prague (then part of Bohemia), Mozart was adored for his music. At the request of the city, he wrote a symphony (No. 38, the 'Prague') and an opera ('Don Giovanni'), some of his best music.

Sequoyah

Around 1770, a Native American Cherokee boy was born in what is now Tennessee in the USA. His name was Sequoyah, 'The Lame One'. Although he could not walk without a limp, Sequoyah didn't let this stop him from achieving his vision. He helped his people through one of the darkest times in their history by giving them the gift of writing.

When Sequoyah grew up, he made silver jewellery for his fellow Cherokees, shod their horses and ran a trading post. He and his wife and children also farmed and raised livestock. They had given up many of their old ways and adopted many of the customs of white people, just as other members of their tribe were doing. White settlers were moving in on all sides, cutting down forests, ploughing the land and killing or driving away the wild animals, while 'white' diseases were decimating the tribe.

All around the once-vast Cherokee nation, whites were demanding that natives give them land. They wanted the native tribes to move farther west, where whites hadn't yet settled. Some Cherokees had done just that, and now there was an eastern and a western branch of the nation. They hardly ever heard from one another unless a traveller brought news.

Sequoyah's contacts with white people introduced him to books and writing. He observed that, with these 'talking leaves', whites could pass on wisdom and speak to each other across distances. Sequoyah's people had always used their rich store of tales, rituals and symbols – and memory devices like wampum belts – to pass on their wisdom, but times were changing. He decided that his people needed talking leaves too. Then the Eastern and Western Cherokees could reunite and save their traditional teachings.

Without ever learning to read or even speak English, Sequoyah spent twelve years developing a Cherokee writing system. He borrowed symbols from the whites' alphabet and then added some he had made up. He first thought to make each symbol represent a different word, but that was too complicated. So he developed a simpler approach where each symbol represented a different syllable. It had eighty-six symbols and was completely phonetic, with no complex spelling rules. It represented the actual sounds of the Cherokee language, which the white alphabet could not do.

During these years, Sequoyah's fellow Cherokees ridiculed him for his efforts. Some thought he had gone crazy. But when he was ready, he persuaded the Cherokee National Council to watch a demonstration.

In 1821, Sequoyah's six-year-old daughter read aloud to the Council chiefs from a letter she had never seen before. Within a few hours, Sequoyah had also taught several young men to read. The chiefs immediately realised the value of his 'syllabary'. They launched a campaign to spread Cherokee writing. It was so easy to learn that people could teach others straight after they had learned it. A whole nation became literate within months.

Using Sequoyah's invention, the chiefs then began a campaign to preserve Cherokee rights to their homelands. In 1828, Sequoyah helped the chiefs draw up a Cherokee constitution written in Cherokee. It was modelled on the US Constitution. That same year, a Cherokee newspaper using his syllabary began publication. Sequoyah also represented his people in Washington, DC. Around this time, he was moved to Arkansas territory, where he taught many Western Cherokees how to read and write.

To drive off their now peaceable Cherokee neighbours, white settlers repeatedly attacked and burned their homes and killed or enslaved them.

However, the efforts of the Cherokees to preserve their nation could not hold back the tide of white settlers. In 1838, the Cherokees were forcibly removed from their homelands and resettled on a reservation far to the west, in a strange new land. Sequoyah did not give up, however. Until his disappearance in Mexico in 1843, he continued to travel among his people, teaching them how to read and write. They used their literacy to stay in touch with each other and to begin rebuilding their lives.

Although the Cherokee syllabary is no longer in use, Sequoyah's name did find immortality. The giant California sequoia trees, among the largest and oldest living things on earth, bear his name, a tribute to his vision of a strong and lasting Cherokee people.

A UNITED NATION

When Europeans arrived in North America, they regarded the natives as primitive savages. They thought their religion, their ideas and their artefacts (like guns, ploughs, wheels, writing, money) made them more civilised. And they hungered for land in a way that the natives could not understand.

After the American Revolution, immigrants poured into North America looking for a better life. To them wealth meant good farmland. The settlers who filtered into native homelands believed they had a right to use these fertile lands for farming. To them, the land was going to waste, and surely there was plenty for all?

What they didn't realise was that the native way of life blended in with the land. The Cherokees occupied the beautiful mountain areas of what is now the south-eastern United States. They hunted large animals that needed space to roam. They also farmed, and gathered roots, berries and medicinal plants widely scattered in the forests. They cherished their land, the resting place of their beloved ancestors. The idea of owning a little plot of it seemed silly and destructive to them. White settlers unwittingly destroyed the balance of nature and traditional native life.

Wealthy, northern-educated and blue-eyed, John Ross was only one-eighth Cherokee, but he was totally devoted to his tribe.

In addition, the new US government – and unscrupulous individuals – continually made treaties promising to pay for land taken, and to seize no more land. But the payments were not made, and the treaties were always broken, especially after gold was discovered.

As they were slowly pushed off their lands, at first the Cherokees fought back, then sent their children to missionary schools, and some even to the great universities in the Northern states. In addition, they formed themselves into a nation, led by their visionary chief, John Ross, for nearly forty years. John Ross aroused tremendous public support for his people in the Northern states, but not enough to counter hostility to Native Americans in the South. It was the first sign of the divisions that led to the Civil War, when slavery became the main issue.

The united Cherokees fought a long legal battle against the white settlers who were invading their lands. They used the US courts, the press, hard bargaining and non-violent resistance in their battle to stay on their homelands and to remain a nation. In 1829, one lawsuit even reached the US Supreme Court, which decided in their favour. But the US president, Andrew Jackson, refused to enforce the decision.

By then Sequoyah had moved west. But he followed the Cherokees' struggle to keep their homes. More and more of their lands were taken over by new states: Georgia, North Carolina and Tennessee. The final blow came when gold was discovered in Cherokee territory. The US wanted it, and eventually the Cherokees and other tribes were ordered to leave their lands and move west.

Most Cherokees refused. They hid out in the forests and mountains. Whites burned their new villages and seized their belongings, but they still held out, never fighting back. Finally, in 1838, thousands of them were rounded up in surprise raids. Their homes and even the graves of their ancestors were looted, while they were marched off, forced to leave everything behind. Over a quarter of the tribe died of disease, cold and starvation as they were driven west, along what is still called the Trail of Tears.

Resettled in 'Indian Territory', they rebuilt their lives and worked out differences with other displaced tribes, some of them old enemies. They also survived the US Civil War and further invasions by white people. Eventually, the Cherokee nation had to dissolve when 'Indian Territory' became the state of Oklahoma in 1907. But the first Congressmen from the new state were Cherokee, a sign of the tribe's lasting strength and vitality. Given a choice, they would have named the new state Sequoyah.

A MAN WITH A VISION

Sequoyah may not have appreciated how unique his achievement was. Never before nor since in history has one man invented a writing system for a whole people. It usually takes centuries of trial and error to develop writing. Sequoyah did realise that his invention could help other tribes. In his old age he travelled and taught his syllabary to them as well.

We can imagine him hunkered down outside someone's home, surrounded by children and their parents. Perhaps they are not as wealthy as some members of their tribe, but they are eager to learn. He uses a stick to trace syllables in the dirt and pronounces each one carefully. Soon the whole group is practising. Some use knives or charcoal to trace symbols on pieces of bark. Excitedly, they practise writing and reading to each other. After a day or so, he goes to another settlement, in the hope that the great traditions of the native peoples will be preserved.

SEQUOYAH'S NORTH AMERICA

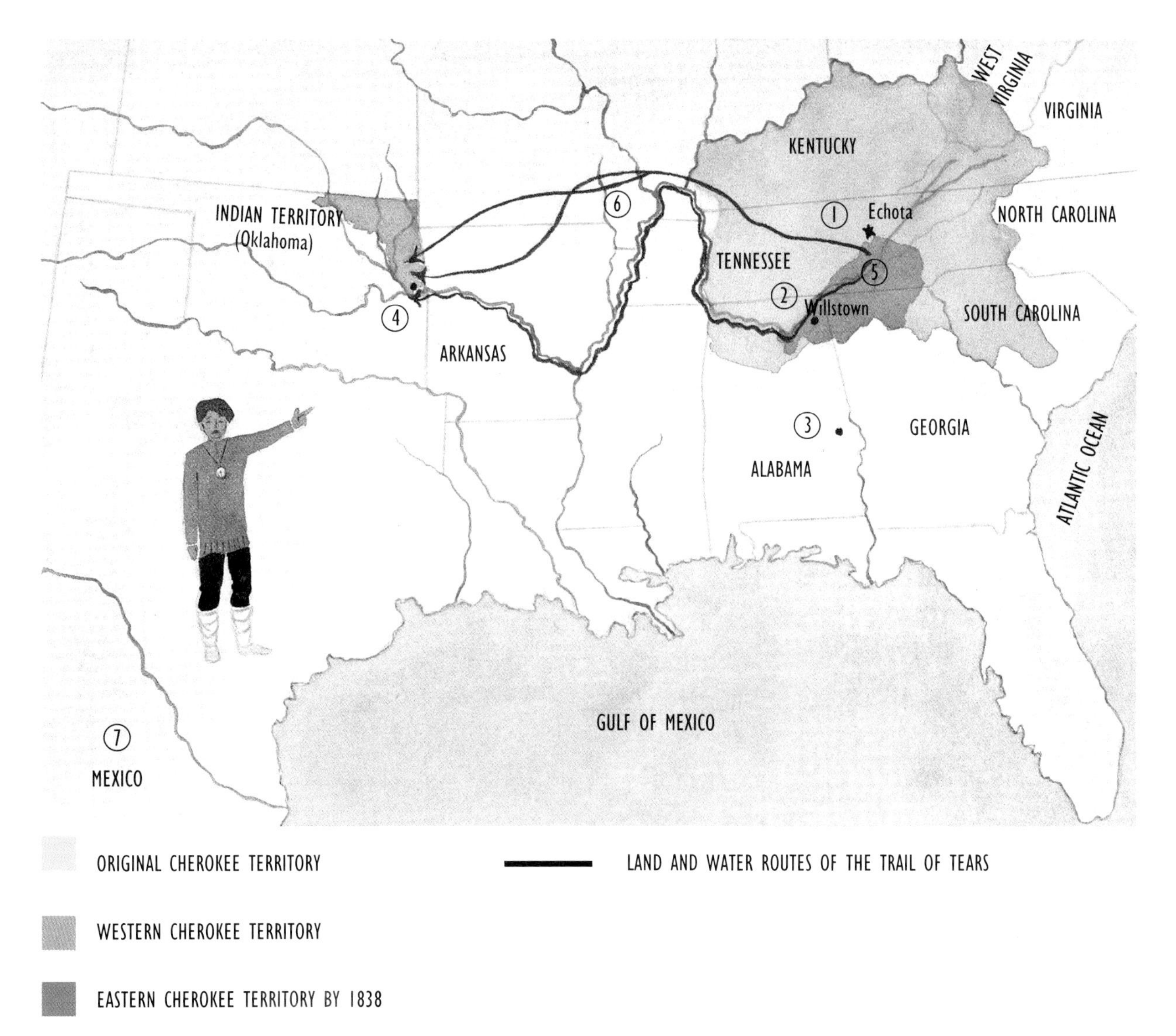

1. Sequoyah was born near the old Cherokee capital of Echota.
2. As a young man, Sequoyah lived in Willstown, working as a silversmith and blacksmith until he moved to Arkansas. He returned to Willstown to demonstrate his syllabary.
3. As allies of the US, Sequoyah and his fellow warriors helped defeat the Creek tribe at the Battle of Horseshoe Bend. They were led by Andrew Jackson, who later betrayed the Cherokees when he was president.
4. In 1818, Sequoyah joined the western Cherokees in Arkansas, continuing to work on his syllabary. He returned there after demonstrating his syllabary to the National Council in 1821.
5. In 1838, about 5,000 Cherokees were rounded up and imprisoned in stockades, where they began to die even before being marched off.
6. John Ross persuaded the US to let the remaining Cherokees organise their own departure, and 13,000 more made the long journey west, during which over a quarter died, including Ross's wife.
7. In 1842, Sequoyah journeyed to Mexico to find more Cherokees rumoured to have settled there. It was here that he died.

Mohandas Gandhi, the Mahatma

To millions of Indians, Mohandas Gandhi was the Mahatma, the 'Great Soul'. Believing that truth and non-violent non-cooperation could be more effective than the use of weapons, Gandhi helped India attain independence from Great Britain without a violent revolution.

Gandhi was born in 1869. Shy and sensitive, he grew up in a traditional Hindu family, where he learned respect for all living things. He also had a stubborn streak that led him to make his own decisions. Breaking with tradition, he left his young wife, Kasturbai, behind in India and went to England to study law. There he discovered and developed a passion for the idea of justice.

Back in India, Gandhi was too shy to be a successful lawyer. He finally found work in South Africa, where non-white people were considered inferior. Indians were often very badly treated there. Soon after he and his family arrived, he was dumped off a train by whites because of his dark skin colour. Gandhi felt so outraged that he vowed to overcome his shyness and change things. He believed that all citizens of the British Empire should be treated as equals.

Gandhi decided to use as his 'weapons' what he called *satyagraha*, 'the force of truth', and *ahimsa*, 'non-harm to others'. He would lead strikes, make speeches and work for justice, but he would never use violence. He would take on the hatred and violence of those who oppressed others, confident that they would eventually give in to truth and justice. He plunged into local politics, founded a newspaper, set up retreat centres where people could learn about *satyagraha*, and led peaceful protest marches. Kasturbai loyally helped him.

Gandhi's successful campaigns for Indians in South Africa made him famous in India and England. He returned to India in the early 1900s, already a trusted leader. He wanted to reform certain aspects of Indian life that he felt weakened India, including raising the status of millions of impoverished peasants and villagers and overcoming hatred between Muslims and Hindus.

Gandhi wanted to reform India as a step towards his greatest goal, Indian independence from Great Britain. After his experiences in South Africa, he no longer believed that the Empire could benefit Indians. He saw that Britain wanted to keep India both politically

and economically dependent. For instance, Indians had once woven their own cloth. Now they were expected to buy mass-produced English cloth instead. Wherever Gandhi went, he taught spinning, so villagers could produce their own cloth. Spinning came to symbolize India's drive for independence.

Just as in Africa, Gandhi founded several ashrams, or religious retreat centres, where people came to study *satyagraha*, and then went home to organise non-violent resistance to British rule.

For almost forty years, Gandhi and his followers campaigned for India's freedom. He led non-violent strikes and marches, fasted and prayed. Repeatedly imprisoned and nearly dying from his fasts, he worked tirelessly to promote freedom and self-reliance for all Indians.

In 1947, India achieved independence, but at a price. Even Gandhi could not bridge the gulf between Hindus and Muslims. As violence exploded, the British government partitioned India into two countries, Hindu India and Muslim Pakistan, thinking it would prevent civil war. Instead, millions of Hindus and Muslims found themselves on the wrong side of the new borders. Fighting broke out on both sides. Gandhi was aghast and, in an attempt to stop the bloodshed, fasted so rigorously that he nearly died. This did indeed help stop some of the fighting as most Indians adored him and wanted him to live.

However, Hindu extremists blamed Gandhi for the partition – and in 1948 one of them assassinated him. Indians were devastated, and people around the world mourned.

THE INDIAN EMPIRE

India is so large, it is called a sub-continent. It stretches across towering mountains, steamy jungles and dusty plains. It supports millions of people whose culture is ancient, rich and varied. It is home to a unique national religion, Hinduism.

India was invaded by Muslim conquerors in the

India's ancient, rich and varied culture seemed exotic and glamorous to the English.

thirteenth century. They ruled many areas of India right up to the twentieth century. By then, the British had taken control, first through trade, then through military might.

India became the 'Jewel in the Crown' of the British Empire. England brought over governors and educators, built an enormous railway system and educated some upper-caste Indians in England, but its main aim was to control India's vast wealth. Half of India's revenues went back to England, while peasants suffered from starvation and were given no education or medical care. In addition, the British divided Indians against each other, often favouring Muslims over Hindus.

According to Hindu tradition, everyone belonged to an hereditary social rank or caste: priest, warrior, tradesman or labourer. But many Hindus were classified as 'outcastes' and labelled 'untouchables'. They could only do work that no one else wanted. They lacked education, health care and decent living conditions. The English saw the caste system as proof of Indian inferiority.

Kasturbai had never met Gandhi before they married, but her deep loyalty to him led her out of a traditional Hindu marriage into the world of politics and social reform.

Indians entered the twentieth century ready for change. They wanted independence, and they wanted to decide for themselves what their country should be like. Gandhi became a focus for India's desire for achieving independence and self-esteem.

Gandhi understood that some aspects of Indian culture did indeed present a problem. For instance, as long as outcastes were treated badly by their own people, the English were bound to feel that they had a right to rule and educate the Indian nation English-style. Calling the outcastes *Harijans*, 'God's Children', Gandhi worked to raise their status.

THE SALT MARCH

One way the British controlled Indians was through monopolising the production and sale of salt. In a hot country like India, a lack of salt in the diet can be fatal. Paying for it was a hardship for the poor. Yet India had salt in abundance on its beaches and in its seas.

Gandhi chose this issue to highlight the unfairness of the British system. In 1930, he decided to walk to the sea from his ashram at Ahmedabad, a distance of almost 250 miles, and make his own salt from sea water. He announced his plans to the press, and began his march with a few followers. Newspapers and radios across the world carried the story of his journey. As word spread, more and more people joined him. By the time he reached the sea at Dandi, twenty-four days later, thousands of people had joined his march.

When Gandhi and his followers began making salt from sea water, they broke the British monopoly. Up and down the coastline of India, people began making their own salt. The salt they collected was not very good, but they proved they could work together peaceably to oppose the British.

More non-violent protests followed. Sometimes the protesters were beaten, and over 60,000 were arrested, but their determination and their willingness to sacrifice themselves finally wore down the British. They repealed the salt laws.

It takes a special kind of greatness to inspire people to risk their lives for a cause, and especially when they commit themselves to non-violence. Gandhi was not only great because of his ideals, but because he was willing to step out of his shyness to stand up for those ideals. His uncompromising gentleness made a deep impression on both English and Indians. Wherever he went, people flocked to him for advice and blessings. To the Indian people, he was not just a politician, he was a saint.

NEW BOUNDARIES OF DIVIDED EMPIRE

1. Mohandas Gandhi was born in Porbandar in 1869.

2. Gandhi grew up in Rajkot and was married to Kasturbai there when they were thirteen.

3. After studying law in London, Gandhi tried working in Bombay. Too shy to try cases, he got a job in South Africa in 1898.

4. Most Indians in South Africa worked on plantations as near-slaves. After being dumped off a train by whites between Durban and Pretoria, Gandhi became determined to defend Indian rights non-violently. He also founded an ashram called Tolstoy Farm, after the great Russian author and pacifist.

5. In 1916, now famous for his work in South Africa, Gandhi returned home and began touring and teaching throughout India. He founded several ashrams, including one at Ahmedabad, from which his Salt March began in 1930.

6. Gandhi and Kasturbai lived in another ashram at Nagpur from 1935 to 1945.

7. Often imprisoned (Kasturbai by his side), such as here at Pune, Gandhi still influenced Indians by fasting nearly to death.

8. In 1947, after the partition of India into India and Pakistan, Gandhi quelled riots in Calcutta – by fasting.

9. Gandhi did the same in Delhi in early 1948, shaming both Hindus and Muslims into calling a truce. However, here he was shot and killed by a Hindu extremist who blamed him for the break-up of India.

BRITAIN'S INDIAN EMPIRE

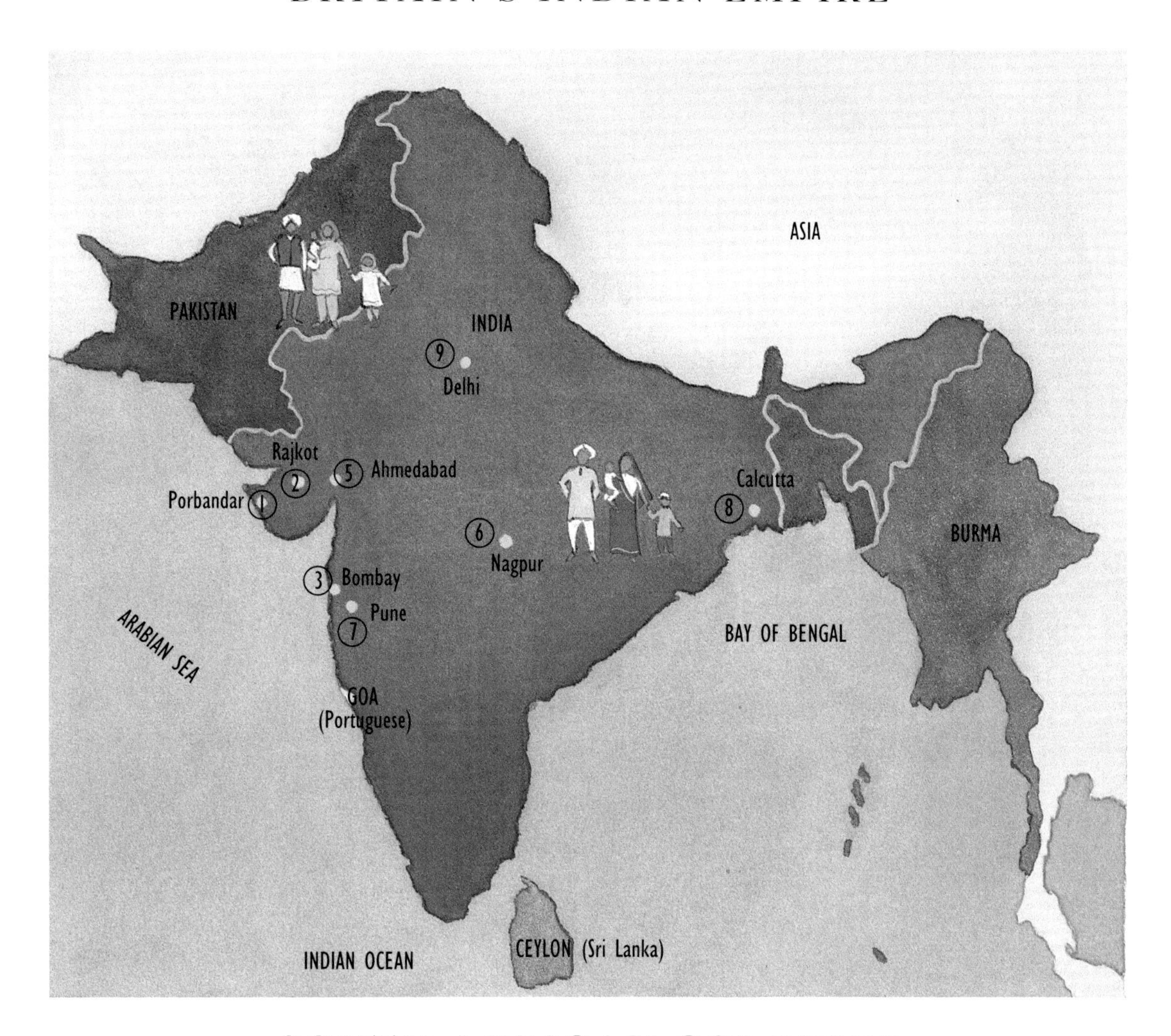

SOUTH AFRICAN COLONIES

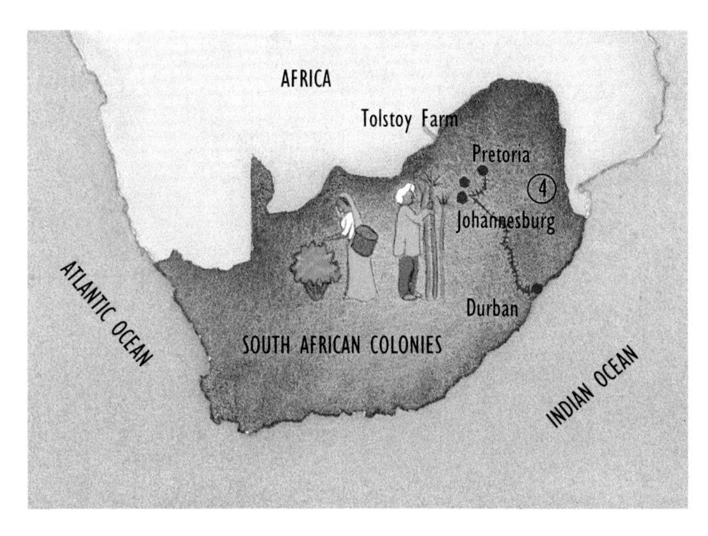

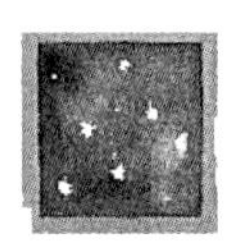

Albert Einstein

Albert Einstein was born in Germany in 1879. As he grew up, everything around him seemed to him both wondrous and puzzling. When he was twelve, he decided to set about solving 'the riddle of the huge world'. In his quest for answers, Einstein revolutionised modern science.

He decided that physics might offer him some understanding of the world. Physics is the study of space, time, matter and energy – everything from the tiniest atomic particles to the greatest galaxies. After completing university, he worked as an office clerk by day and on his own ideas at night. In 1905, when he was twenty-six, Einstein began publishing scientific papers explaining his new theories. Some scientists scoffed at his ideas, especially when they found out he wasn't a university professor. Other scientists were intrigued and tested them for themselves. Their observations confirmed what his theories predicted.

Before Einstein, people had thought space was like a huge, empty container and that time passed even if nothing was happening. They thought that the universe moved separately inside space and time. But there were many things this view couldn't explain. Einstein proposed that time, space and matter are bound up together. Without matter in the universe, space and time would disappear. Einstein added that light is bent by gravity, that space is curved, and that time appears to move more slowly for objects that move faster.

Most people felt that Einstein's new theories could only be understood by fellow scientists, but today many people at least know his famous formula, $E=mc^2$. It relates matter, energy and light to each other. Einstein said that what we see as solid objects are in fact condensed energy. To find an object's energy, multiply the speed of light first by itself and then by the mass of the object. Therefore, E(energy) = m(mass) x c^2(speed of light x itself). Based on his theories, scientists figured out how to split atoms, creating a new world of nuclear power.

Einstein won the Nobel Prize for science in 1921. He also became a scientific superstar, adored the world over. Embarrassed by fame, he kept on searching for a simple law of the universe that could unite all scientific laws. He spent his life seeking it.

At the same time, Einstein and his discoveries were swept into world politics. In 1914, Germany had plunged into World War I. But believing in the unity of humankind, Einstein openly opposed this and all war. He was convinced it only harmed and divided people. Then in the 1920s and 1930s the National Socialist German Workers' Party (the 'Nazis')

$e=(4.774 \pm 0.002 \times 10^{-10}$ esu $E=mc^2$ $E=hv$ $\lambda v=c$ $\lambda=hc/E$
$\lambda_c=h/mc$ $\lambda=h/2\pi mc$ $m=140/c^2$ $c=1.60\times10^{-19}$ $\pi^+\rightarrow\mu^++v_\mu$
$\mu_o^2c^2e^4m_e/8h^3$ $\mu_oce^2/2h=4\pi\times10^{-7}$ $\pi+p\rightarrow+K^++\lambda$
$F=N_Ae$ $V=(2e/h)V$ $\mu\rightarrow e^-+\bar{v}_e+\bar{v}_\mu$

rose to power in Germany. One of their goals was to wipe out 'inferior races', and Jews were their special target. Although he did not practise Judaism, Einstein was born Jewish and became an object of particular hatred. Unable to withstand the Nazi attacks, he moved to the USA, taking a job as a professor at Princeton University in New Jersey.

During World War II, he heard that the Nazis were developing atomic weapons based on his discoveries. He wrote to the President of the United States, warning him. In fact it was the Americans who developed 'atom bombs' first and used them to end World War II, causing horrifying destruction. Einstein had not intended his discoveries for such uses and regretted his part in their creation. Feeling that 'we have won the war, but we have not won the peace', he spent the rest of his life working not only for science but for world peace.

As a boy, Einstein loved to walk in the country, taking in the mystery and wonder of nature.

A WORLD DIVIDED

Throughout Europe's history, Jews have been persecuted by Christians. When the Nazi leader Adolf Hitler came to power in Germany, he made Jews into scapegoats for all Germany's ills. He encouraged people to hate and fear Jews, claiming they were of a different, inferior race from other Europeans. He tried to discredit Einstein and his 'Jewish' theories, even though Nazi scientists used them in war research. Hitler claimed that Germans were a pure 'master race' destined to rule the world. He wanted to kill off not only Jews but other so-called inferior races. His list included Gypsies, Catholics, and anyone who opposed him.

As persecution of Jews increased, Einstein came to believe that Jews must leave Europe and re-found their ancient homeland in Palestine, in the Near East. They had been exiled from Palestine by the Romans 2000 years earlier. Many had moved back and built settlements, but Palestine, under Turkish rule until 1918, was now under British rule.

Hitler triggered World War II and thousands of Jews fled Europe. In the United States, Einstein used his influence to help these refugees. After World War II ended, the world learned that Hitler's Nazis had murdered millions of people, including more than six million Jews.

The Allies who had fought against Hitler agreed that the Jews must be given back their ancient homeland as a way to heal the deep wounds caused by the war and provide a secure base for them. The new Jewish state of Israel was founded in 1948 in the land of Palestine. The first prime minister, David Ben Gurion, asked Einstein to come to Israel to be its president. Although he felt honoured, Albert Einstein refused; he was a scientist, not a politician.

Unfortunately, Einstein's dream of a Jewish nation met with many obstacles. Israel was founded against the wishes of the Arab people already living there. War erupted again, this time between the new Israeli state and its neighbours. Einstein passed away while this new conflict continued, still hoping for a world where people could realise they are all related, just as matter and energy are.

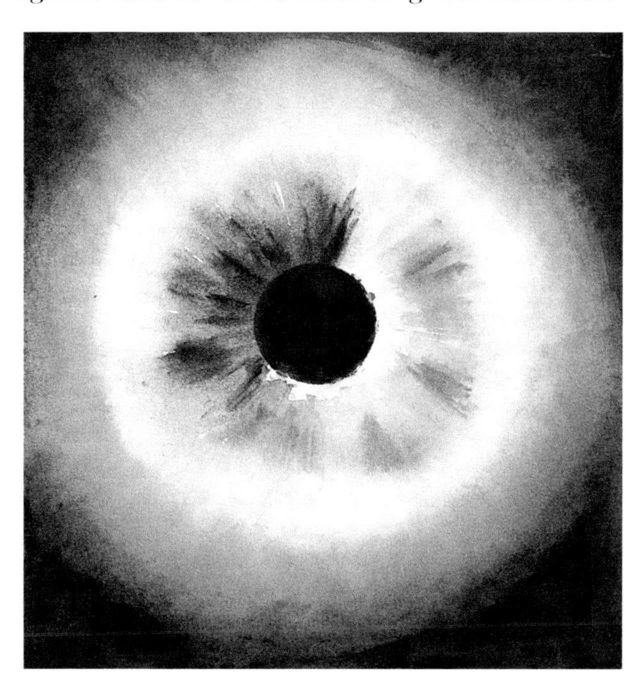

In 1919, English scientists tested Einstein's theory of relativity by observing a total solar eclipse in Africa and Brazil. They proved his predictions were correct: starlight is bent by the sun's gravity!

EINSTEIN'S IMAGINATION

Nowadays, when we call someone a genius, we often say they are an 'Einstein'. However, Albert Einstein often got poor grades as a result of the strict, regimented teaching he received at school. One of his teachers said he would never amount to anything. They didn't understand his creative imagination, which he used in all his studies. When he was sixteen, he dreamed of riding on a beam of light. That experience gave him his first insight into relativity and led him to study physics at university.

After leaving university, Einstein continued to study and think about physics. When observing something, he imagined what it would do under different conditions. Then he worked out his theories mathematically and made predictions about how things should work if those theories were true. For instance, traditionally the word 'mass' had been used in two different ways. One kind of mass (inertial mass) results in resistance when objects are pushed. Another type of mass (gravitational mass) is defined as the gravitational force between two bodies. Within his theory of relativity, Einstein stated that both kinds of mass are the same. He maintained that, if that was true, the two aspects of mass would cancel each other out in a falling object. In this way, people falling from a great height would feel weightless. You can test this part of his theory for yourself when you ride a roller coaster.

Einstein also stated that there is no such thing as absolute time. He suggested that time is experienced differently for objects moving relative to one another. For instance, to people flying in a spaceship, the ship seems to stand still while the earth appears to be moving away. But people on earth see the ship moving away and feel the earth is standing still. To someone on earth, the clocks on the ship would seem to move more slowly than those on earth, while to those on the ship the clocks on earth would seem to move more slowly. It would be no good asking which time is the true time!

Einstein changed the way we see our world. Yet he had trouble accepting the changes his theories brought about. Not only did other scientists invent atomic weapons, they used his theories to explore the unpredictable, indeterminate qualities of our world. Einstein intensely disliked their ideas, and found himself more and more isolated from new scientific developments. Yet he continued to attract world attention as he tried to discover a new unifying law of the universe.

Einstein died without ever finding a unifying law of the universe, but he changed the entire direction of modern physics. Inspired by his example, scientists are still trying to solve 'the riddle of the huge world'.

EINSTEIN IN EUROPE

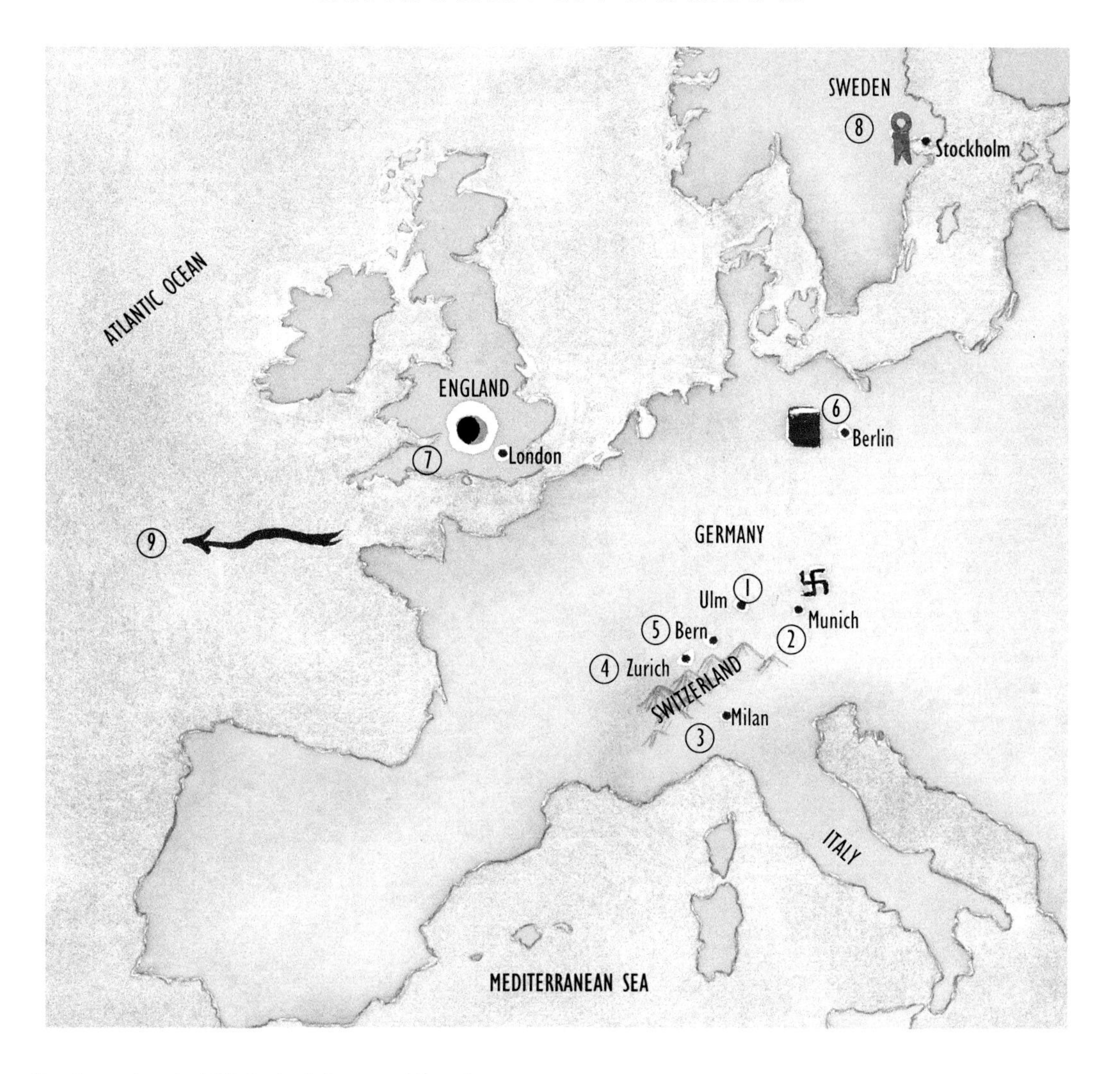

1. Albert Einstein was born in 1879, in the little town of Ulm, Germany.
2. When Einstein was a baby, his family moved to Munich, where he grew up.
3. Einstein dropped out of school and followed his family to Milan, Italy, when he was fifteen.
4. Soon he was back at school, in Zurich, Switzerland. Graduating from university in 1900, he became a Swiss citizen.
5. Unable to get a university professorship, he worked in the Swiss Patent Office in Bern, continued studying on his own and published his theories in scientific journals.
6. By 1914, Einstein was already respected in the scientific community and had become a university professor. He settled in Berlin, where he witnessed Germany enthusiastically plunging into war.
7. In 1919, the Royal Society in London announced its findings from a solar eclipse in Africa and Brazil, thereby proving Einstein's theory of relativity to be correct. He became famous overnight, and began travelling and teaching around the world.
8. Einstein received the Nobel Prize at Stockholm in 1921, but in pre-Nazi Germany he found himself increasingly under suspicion as an outspoken pacifist and a Jew.
9. By 1933, he finally had to leave Germany, accepting a position at Princeton University in the USA. There, in 1939, he wrote to President Roosevelt, warning him that Nazi Germany might be developing nuclear weapons, and there he died in 1955.

Jorge Luis Borges

'...dreaming is my task ... I am astonished at things'

Born in Buenos Aires, Argentina, Jorge Luis Borges inherited two worlds. One was the land and culture of Argentina: great mountains and plains, rivers, jungles and deserts; gauchos, the tango, a European outlook and revolutionary patriotism. The other was the world of books and dreams. In his writing, Borges merged the two together to become one of the greatest Spanish-language authors of the twentieth century.

Borges was born in 1899. As a boy, he was shy and nearsighted. His famous ancestors had fought for Argentine freedom, but he was a target for bullies. He couldn't fight like they did, so he read and wrote about imaginary worlds. There his weakness didn't count.

Borges' family moved to Europe when he was a teenager. When World War I erupted, they had to stay in Switzerland until it ended. Reading on his own, Borges discovered myths, adventures and mysteries from around the world. They echoed his feeling that life is mysterious and sometimes frightening, but always magical.

After the war ended, Borges and his family went to Spain. There he became friends with other young writers. They hated the long-winded, stylised writing that was popular at the time, and wanted to create a bolder, simpler Spanish literature. Borges had a flair for writing in this new way.

When his family returned to Buenos Aires in 1921, Borges introduced this new movement to Argentina. He wrote poems, essays and short stories, edited magazines and books, and translated famous works of literature into Spanish. His readers enjoyed his gentle wit and wide-ranging imagination.

However, Borges' eyesight was beginning to fail. In 1938, he struck his head against the corner of an open casement window. The wound became infected and he nearly died. He was unable to speak for a while, and was terrified he would not be able to write again. When he recovered from his injury, Borges began to write in a way that combined realism, science fiction, fantasy and history. Some were funny and others were eerie, but they always blurred the line between dreaming and waking, fantasy and reality. This style became popular throughout Latin America and is now referred to as 'magical realism'.

Borges' writing income couldn't support him, and he was too shy to lecture or teach as other authors did. Instead, despite his increasing blindness, he worked in a library. There his

fellow workers didn't know about his writing career. They didn't even recognise him when they saw an article about him in an encyclopedia.

Wider fame came to Borges in the 1940s with the rise of a powerful dictator, Juan Perón. Borges was not interested in politics, but he had criticised Perón's support for the Nazis and their allies. In revenge, Perón tried to humiliate him. He briefly imprisoned Borges' mother and sister. Then he took away Borges' library job and 'promoted' him to Inspector of Chickens and Rabbits, implying he was a coward. Instead, Borges turned to full-time writing, editing, and even began lecturing on literature, which truly terrified him. But he did become a hero to those who opposed Perón. After Perón's downfall in the 1950s, the Argentine government honoured Borges, making him Director of the National Library.

By now, he was completely blind, but he kept 'writing', dictating his work to others. In his sixties, Borges suddenly became world famous when he received a major literary award, the Formentor Prize. Universities around the world invited him to teach. He received honours wherever he went, and was idolised by a new generation of readers across Europe and the US. Unaffected by fame, Borges continued to dream, to write and to be astonished by the world around him.

BORGES' ARGENTINA

Like many countries in South America, Argentina was once part of a huge area claimed by Spain. As in North America, settlers in Argentina expelled or killed most of the natives, leaving little trace of their culture. In the early nineteenth century, the territory containing Argentina revolted against Spain. After winning independence, it split into the countries of Bolivia, Uruguay, Paraguay and Argentina.

With its rich lands and varied climate, Argentina soon attracted settlers from all over the world. They set up huge cattle and sheep ranches, farmed the

Borges romanticised the lives of Argentinian cowboys, or gauchos, just as North Americans romanticise their cowboys.

Borges loved the music and lyrics of the tango, a dance of passion, though he himself led a quiet life.

pampas (plains), built railways, manufactured goods to export, and prospered. Spanish remained the national language, but other European and Oriental peoples contributed to a culture that recognised many different backgrounds.

With such diversity, Argentinians have generally been tolerant of each other. They pride themselves on their high level of education and artistic achievement. Reading is one of their many passions, and writers deeply influence their thinking.

Argentinians have suffered from unstable governments from the time they gained independence. Although Argentina's constitution was modelled upon the US Constitution, and human rights were guaranteed, the country has often been ruled by military dictators. Thus no leader could survive without the support of powerful generals.

Juan Perón was such a dictator. He stifled many constitutional freedoms, while buying popularity with social programmes. Many Argentinians adored his beautiful wife, Eva.

After her death, he tried to have her declared a saint. She has even become the basis for a world-famous musical called *Evita*. But Perón had nearly bankrupted the country and was finally overthrown. Still, Perónism continues to fascinate Argentinians, who have suffered even worse political oppression by later dictators.

As with many Argentinians, Borges' ancestry was mixed. His was part Spanish, Portuguese, Italian and English. He blended a European outlook with pride in his country's heritage. He was fascinated with the romantic gauchos, legendary cowboys of the pampas. He loved the colourful language of the streets – *lunfardo*. A secret code-slang developed by gangsters, it substituted vivid imagery for proper names. For instance, someone's head might be called a ball or a roof. This language inspired not only Borges and other writers, but songwriters too. Argentina's famous dance, the tango, was born out of *lunfardo*.

His writing mixed these Argentine elements with references to literature from around the world, and with dreams and events from his own life. He was a great scholar, and he could write in a bookish way when it suited him. But then he would hide little jokes in his apparently serious essays. For instance, he would write a book review – of a book never written. He would mix up quotes from real and imaginary books. People would want to read these made-up books, only to find they didn't exist. This kind of play was part of his way of expressing how our lives are made up from our imagination. Often our imagination seems to match the world, but it can also mislead us, making life seem unreal. Borges wanted people to really see, feel and be astonished by their lives, whether waking or dreaming.

THE BLIND POET

You are sitting all alone in a room. Warm sunshine streams in through an open window and a light breeze stirs the curtains. Outside, you can sometimes hear traffic noises, children playing, or the sound of footsteps. Inside, a clock ticks in the next room. As you sit, the noises from outside die away. The sun sets and the room grows cooler. Little seems to be going on, no moment stands out as special, but you are not bored.

Borges spent many days of his life like this. He could tell day from night, but he could not see. Instead, he listened to his world and felt its changes through his other senses. He dreamed, composed poetry, remembered past conversations, and waited patiently for visitors. He did not mind waiting. It was part of the astonishment he felt at simply being alive.

BORGES IN ARGENTINA AND EUROPE

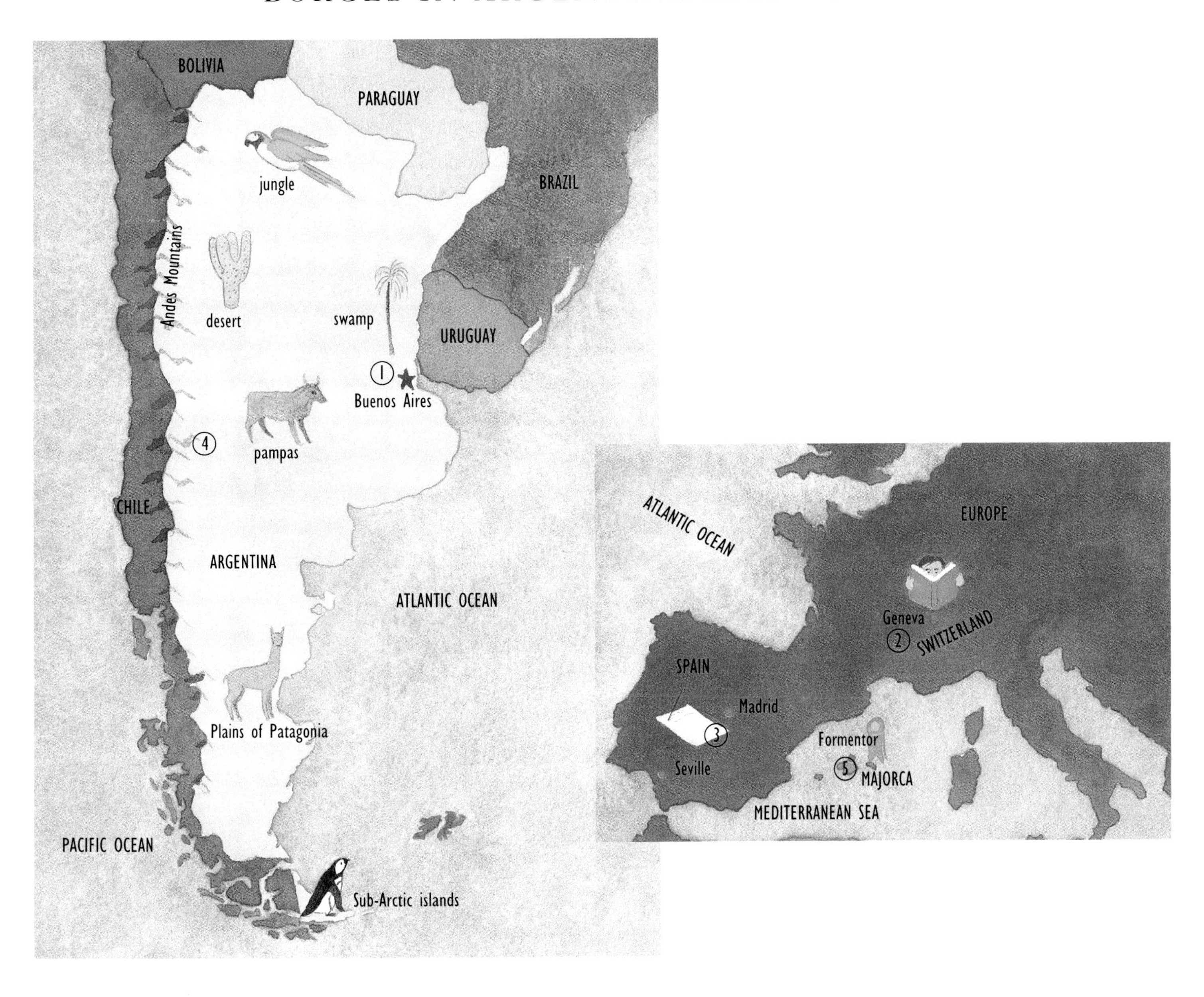

1. Borges was born in Buenos Aires in 1899 and lived most of his life there.

2. When Borges was fourteen, his family moved to Switzerland, where they spent World War I. Here Borges studied languages and world literature, and developed a love of mystery and fantasy.

3. On their way home after the war, the Borges family stayed in Spain for a year. Borges made friends with a group of young poets, taking their ideas with him when he returned to Argentina in 1921.

4. In addition to European literature, the traditions of Argentina influenced Borges' writing. He became popular throughout the country, although at one point he had to endure indignities from the dictator Juan Perón.

5. In 1961, Borges and another author, Samuel Beckett, received the Formentor Prize, awarded by publishers from fourteen countries. He suddenly found himself famous and travelled the world, receiving more awards and honours from different countries until his death in 1986.

Martin Luther King, Junior

Martin Luther King, Junior, was the hero of a civil rights movement in the USA. He led many thousands of people in non-violent protests and resistance against racial discrimination. He raised black people's sense of pride while appealing to the goodness and sense of justice that all people share.

King was born in Atlanta, Georgia, in 1929. His minister father combined religion with a sense of social justice. Throughout the Southern states of the US, racial segregation was the law – black people were not allowed to go to the same school, live in the same neighbourhoods, or even drink from the same water fountains as whites. His loving family protected young Martin from some kinds of racism, and made sure he knew his worth. Still, he grew up thinking the worst of white people, many of whom treated blacks with contempt and even cruelty.

Not until King went to university in the North did he realise that not all white people were racist. He decided that Southern racism was kept alive by unjust laws which must be changed. Then white people could overcome their mistaken attitudes. Blacks were already making some gains: in 1954, the Supreme Court would declare school segregation illegal.

At university King also learned about Mahatma Gandhi's teachings of love and non-violent resistance. Like Gandhi, he felt that there was no difference between spiritual longing and a desire for social justice. Gandhi's teachings showed him how he could work as a pastor to join these two ideals. Instead of staying safely in the North, King and his wife, Coretta, returned south, where they could work for civil rights.

When he became a pastor in Montgomery, Alabama, King was soon thrust into leadership. An incident there sparked a nationwide civil rights movement. When riding on buses, blacks had to sit in the back and give up their seats to whites on demand. In 1955, one black woman refused to get up and, as a result, was arrested. King and other black ministers and leaders organised a successful black boycott of the Montgomery buses that lasted over a year. The case of bus segregation went to the Supreme Court, which once again declared segregation illegal.

Nevertheless, governments of the Southern states ignored its ruling. To push them along, King chose to follow Gandhi's methods. Non-violent resistance must be based on loving one's opponents. King and his supporters practised civil disobedience in the name of higher justice,

and were always ready to go to prison, to be beaten, even to be killed. They did not give in to hatred or try to triumph over white people. King believed that this approach would eventually awaken their sense of justice.

For the next thirteen years, King and others led people across the south, and then across the nation, in non-violent boycotts, sit-ins, marches and demonstrations. As the civil rights movement spread, King raised the hopes and the pride of black people. His eloquent speeches moved both blacks and whites to join the crusade for civil rights. Together, they faced not just arrest but bombings, shootings, lynchings and beatings by those opposed to integration. Watching television, shocked Americans saw policemen beat unarmed people, and turn fire hoses and guard dogs upon them. Many began demanding change. In 1964, the US Congress passed strong civil rights laws and started to enforce them.

Even as newlyweds, the Kings knew the dangers they would face. After her husband's death, Coretta King continued the campaign for civil rights.

Meanwhile, King looked for the underlying causes of black powerlessness and poverty. He campaigned for equal education and job opportunities, registration for voters, and for a sense of black community and pride. He travelled tirelessly, working twenty hours a day, seven days a week.

Always the target for hatred, King was assassinated in 1968. His death seemed like a victory for violence, especially when blacks reacted by rioting in several cities. But King had never flinched from the violence he knew lay in everyone, black and white. He once said, 'If you are cut down in a movement that is designed to save the soul of a nation, then no other death could be more redemptive.' His dream did not die with him, and today people continue working to realise the community he dreamt of.

THE JOURNEY TO FREEDOM

In 1863, in the middle of a devastating civil war between Northern and Southern states, US president Abraham Lincoln issued the Emancipation Proclamation, which outlawed slavery. Although the North and South had been at war for years, and Lincoln opposed slavery, he had hoped that the South would give it up voluntarily. He finally realised that slavery would never end in that way.

After the Civil War, defeated and angry, white Southerners were not ready to alter their relationship with black people. Although free in theory, blacks soon found that little had changed. Whites still ran things, and within fifty years they had passed a series of laws known as 'Jim Crow' laws (after a white song-and-dance routine that demeaned blacks), which were meant to keep black people poor, ignorant and subservient. From going to poorer schools, to having to walk miles to find a blacks-only public lavatory, to being refused service in all-white restaurants, blacks were shut out of a normal life and kept from the prosperity many whites took for granted. Even in the North, black people often lived unofficially segregated in poorer neighbourhoods.

As well as having few chances for obtaining education and wealth, Southern blacks were treated badly at every turn. For almost a hundred years after the Civil War, some whites tried to justify their attitudes by claiming that black people were naturally lazy or stupid. They contemptuously called black men 'boys' and all blacks 'niggers'. Many blacks lost any sense of self-worth. Others stood up for themselves, only to meet with violence. In the South, white supremacist groups like the Ku Klux Klan lynched and beat people, and bombed their homes and churches, while police and judges looked the other way.

Even after the US Supreme Court declared segregated schools illegal in 1954, and bus segregation illegal in 1955, segregation still held sway in the South. For instance, unless forced to integrate by federal troops, white politicians and police refused to allow black children into white schools. There simply were not enough troops to enforce integration everywhere.

Despite such obstacles, blacks still managed to improve their

In 1963, young black children from Birmingham, Alabama, marched to protest about segregation. Police set dogs on them and firemen sprayed them with hoses, sparking national outrage.

lives and work for change. Martin Luther King, Junior, was part of a rising generation that was better off and better educated. His father had gone from penniless sharecropper's son to well-educated minister through his own efforts. People like King felt an even better world was possible for their children, and they were willing to give their lives for that vision. They knew that while federal troops could enforce laws against racism, only mutual respect and personal commitment could change people's hearts.

As the years passed from the 1950s to 1960s, King's philosophy was often attacked by extremists, who either thought he was pushing ahead too fast or not fast enough. It took all of his courage to stand clearly behind the principles of love and non-violence. He often reminded his supporters not to hate other people, but only their wrong actions. He firmly believed that all people had goodness in them, and that it could be awakened by taking on their fear and hatred without giving in to it oneself. His philosophy and commitment earned him the Nobel Peace Prize in 1964. At thirty-five, he was the youngest person ever to receive it.

I HAVE A DREAM

'I have a dream' was a phrase from King's most famous speech. He gave it at the end of a rally in 1963, in Washington, DC. Standing in front of the Lincoln Memorial, he had expected to speak to 100,000 people. Instead, 250,000 people showed up from all over the country. They listened to him spellbound, with tears in their eyes, as he painted a picture in words of a world where all people lived in harmony with each other.

King knew how to speak from the heart and how to inspire the same feeling in others. He had grown up in a Church tradition that allowed people to express their inspiration openly and joyously, and he used that tradition in his civil rights speeches. He had a beautiful deep voice, and he used vivid images to describe his ideas. Some of his speeches came close to poetry or song. He often quoted other great thinkers, in a way that brought their ideas to life. While he treasured his own heritage, he spoke as an educated Southern black man who shared an even greater human heritage with everyone.

As he grew older, King recognised the vastness of what he was trying to achieve. He saw African and Asian nations gaining independence from white colonialist nations, and he saw the black struggle for rights as part of a worldwide awakening. He believed that a new world was being born, and his dream was not that any one race would triumph over another, but that all races, religions and ways of life could be appreciated as different expressions of the same human dignity. His dream still lives.

KING'S CAMPAIGNS FOR CIVIL RIGHTS IN THE USA

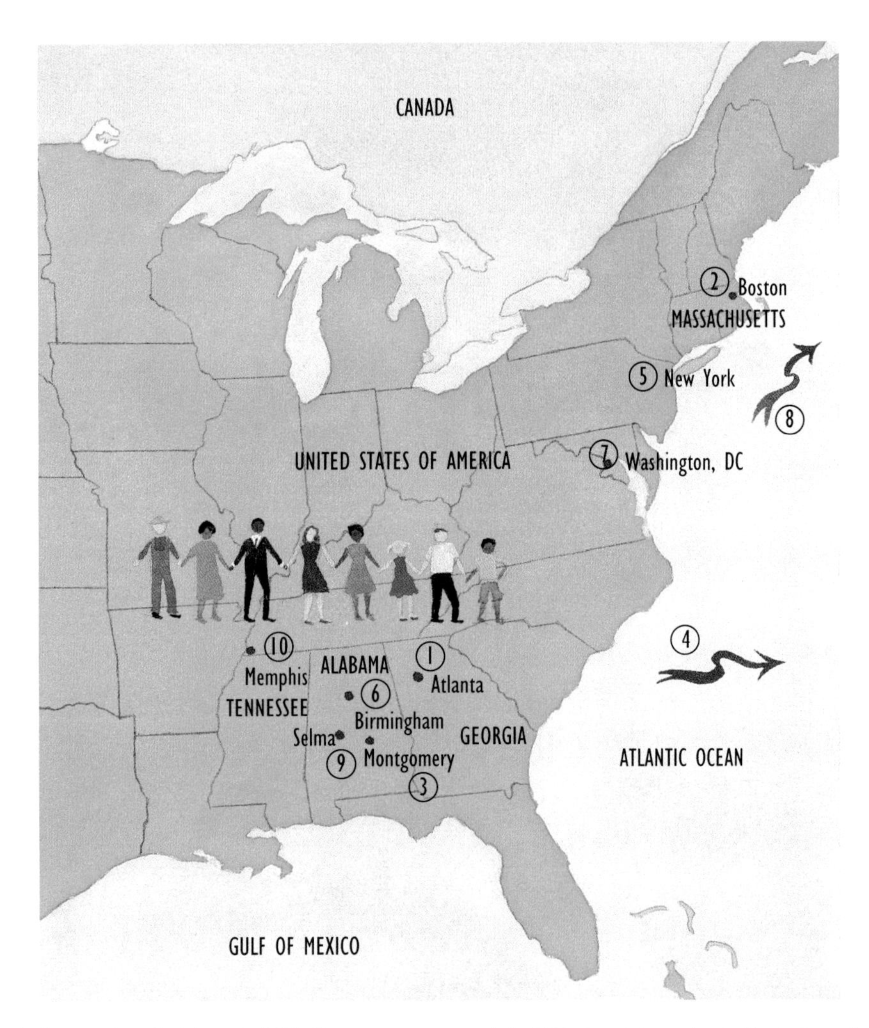

1. Martin Luther King, Junior, was born in Atlanta in 1929. He was ordained as a minister when he was only eighteen.

2. In 1951, after graduating from college, King moved to Boston to continue his education. There he met Coretta; they married in 1953.

3. The Kings moved to Montgomery in 1954, the same year the Supreme Court ruled school segregation unconstitutional. In 1955, King and other ministers began the successful year-long boycott of the bus system.

4. In 1957, the Kings travelled to Ghana and witnessed the growing independence movement in Africa. In 1959, they also travelled to India to pay homage to Mahatma Gandhi.

5. In 1958, while in New York on a book tour, King was stabbed and nearly killed by a deranged black woman – the strangest of the many attempts on his life.

6. In 1963, King led marches in Birmingham, Alabama. After he and all adult protesters were jailed, school children, some as young as six, marched in their stead.

7. That same year, King spoke at a mass rally in Washington, DC, attended by 250,000 people from across the country.

8. In 1964, King received the Nobel Peace Prize at Stockholm. That same year, Congress finally passed strong civil rights laws, and in 1965 they added a new voting rights law.

9. In 1965, after enduring beatings and arrests, King and his supporters from throughout the US marched from Selma to Montgomery to support voting rights for black people.

10. King widened his campaign to include finding jobs and aid for poor people, black and white. He was planning a Poor People's march in Washington in 1968 when, only days before it was due to begin, he was shot and killed in Memphis, Tennessee.

Further Reading

All the titles with an * beside them are written for young people. The ones with an ! are my favourites.

Socrates

Arnott, Peter D. *An Introduction to the Greek World* Macmillan & Co., London and St Martin's Press, New York 1967

*Bowra, C. M. *Classical Greece* Time-Life Books, New York 1965

Green, Peter *Ancient Greece: An Illustrated History* Viking Press, New York 1973

*Mason, Cora *Socrates: The Man Who Dared to Ask* Beacon Press, Boston 1953

*More, Daisy and Bowman, John *Clash of East and West: The Persians, Imperial Greece* Cassell, London and Macmillan Publishing Co., New York 1980

Starr, Chester G. *The Ancient Greeks* Oxford University Press, New York 1971

*Taylor, Duncan *Ancient Greece* Methuen & Co., London 1964

Prince Taishi Shotoku

Dilts, Marion *The Pageant of Japanese History* David McKay Co., New York 1961

Packard, Jerrold M. *Sons of Heaven: A Portrait of the Japanese Monarchy* Charles Scribner & Sons, New York 1987

Reischauer, Edwin and Fairbank, John *East Asia: The Great Tradition* Houghton Mifflin Co., Boston 1960

Mansa Kankan Musa

Atmore, Anthony and Stacey, Gillian *Black Kingdoms Black Peoples* G. P. Putnam & Sons, New York 1979

*Chu, Daniel and Skinner, Elliott *A Glorious Age in Africa* Africa World Press, Trenton 1992

Fage, J. D. *A History of West Africa* Cambridge University Press, Cambridge 1969

Levitzion, Nehemiah *Ancient Ghana and Mali* Methuen & Co., London 1973

*McKissack, Patricia and Fredrich *The Royal Kingdoms of Ghana, Mali, and Songhay* Henry Holt & Co., New York 1994

Leonardo da Vinci

Calder, Ritchie *Leonardo and the Age of the Eye* Simon & Schuster, New York 1970

!Clark, Kenneth *Leonardo da Vinci* Cambridge University Press, Cambridge 1952

Heydenreich, Ludwig, Dibner, Bern and Reti, Ladislao *Leonardo the Inventor* McGraw-Hill Book Co./Hutchinson, London 1981

*Keele, Kenneth *Leonardo da Vinci and the Art of Science* Wayland Publishers, Hove 1977

*!McLanathan, Richard *Leonardo da Vinci* Harry N. Abrams, New York 1990

!Reti, Ladislao (ed.) *The Unknown Leonardo* McGraw-Hill Book Co., New York 1974

*Sachs, Marianne *Leonardo and His World* Ward Lock, London 1979

*Skira-Venturi, Rosabianca *A Weekend with Leonardo da Vinci* Rizzoli International Publications, New York 1993

William Shakespeare

!Brown, Ivor *Shakespeare in His Time* Thomas Nelson & Sons, Edinburgh 1960

Burgess, Anthony *Shakespeare* Clarke, Irwin & Co., Toronto 1970

Fido, Martin *Shakespeare* Hamlyn Publishing Group, London 1978

Frye, Roland *Shakespeare's Life and Times: A Pictorial Record* Princeton University Press, Princeton 1967

*Martin, Christopher *Shakespeare* Wayland Publishers, Hove 1988

*!Ross, Stewart *Shakespeare and Macbeth* Penguin Books, London 1994

Schoenbaum, S. *Shakespeare: The Globe and the World* Folger Shakespeare Library, Oxford University Press, New York 1979

*!Stanley, Diane *Bard of Avon: The Story of William Shakespeare* Morrow Junior Books, New York 1992

Wright, Louis B. *Shakespeare for Everyone* Washington Square Press, New York 1965

Benjamin Franklin

The Autobiography of Benjamin Franklin Franklin Watts, New York

*Daugherty, James *Poor Richard* Viking Press, New York 1941

*Davidson, Margaret *Benjamin Franklin: Amazing American* Dell Publishing Co., New York 1988

*!Davies, Eryl *Benjamin Franklin: Experimenter Extraordinary* Wayland Publishers, Hove 1981

*Donovan, Frank R. *The Many Worlds of Benjamin Franklin* American Heritage Publishing Co., New York 1963

Fleming, Thomas *Benjamin Franklin* Four Winds Press, New York 1973

*!Metzer, Milton *Benjamin Franklin: The New American* Franklin Watts, New York 1988

Wolfgang Amadeus Mozart

*Downing, Julie *Mozart Tonight* Macmillan Publishing Co., New York 1994

Hutchings, Arthur *Mozart: The Man, the Musician* Thames and Hudson, London 1976

*Komroff, Manuel *Mozart* Alfred A. Knopf, New York 1956

*!Krull, Kathleen *Lives of the Musicians: Good Times, Bad Times* Harcourt Brace Jovanovitch, San Diego 1993

Robbins Landon, H. C. *Mozart: The Golden Years, 1781–1791* Schirmer Books, New York 1989

Sequoyah

*Coblentz, Catherine Cate *Sequoya* Longmans, Green & Co., New York 1954

!* Klauser, Janet, *Sequoyah's Gift* HarperCollins Publishers, New York 1993.

Malone, Henry Thompson *Cherokees of the Old South* University of Georgia Press, Athens (USA) 1956

*!Marriott, Alice *Sequoyah, Leader of the Cherokees* Random House, New York 1956

Van Every, Dale *Disinherited* William Morrow & Co., New York 1966

Woodward, Grace Steele *The Cherokees* University of Oklahoma Press, Norman 1969

Mohandas Gandhi, the Mahatma

Attenborough, Richard *In Search of Gandhi* Bodley Head, London 1982

Coolidge, Olivia *Gandhi* Houghton Mifflin Co., Boston 1971

Gold, Gerald *Gandhi: A Pictorial Biography* Newmarket Press, New York 1983

*Rawding, F. W. *Gandhi and the Struggle for India's Independence* Cambridge University Press, Cambridge 1980

*Spin, Kathryn *Gandhi* Hamish Hamilton, London 1984

Albert Einstein

Calder, Nigel *Einstein's Universe* BBC, London 1979

Highfield, Roger and Carter, Paul *The Private Lives of Albert Einstein* Faber & Faber, London 1993

*Hunter, Nigel *Einstein* Wayland Publishers, Hove 1986

*Reef, Catherine *Albert Einstein, Scientist of the 20th Century* Dillon Press, Minneapolis 1991

Jorge Luis Borges

*!Gofen, Ethel Caro *Argentina* Marshall Cavendish Corporation, New York 1992

Monegal, Emir Rodriguez *Jorge Luis Borges: A Literary Biography* E. P. Dutton, New York 1978

Martin Luther King, Junior

*Clayton, Ed *Martin Luther King: The Peaceful Warrior* Prentice Hall, New York 1971

*Davidson, Margaret *I Have a Dream: The Story of Martin Luther King* Scholastic, New York 1986

*!Jakoubeck, Robert *Martin Luther King, Jr.* Chelsea House Publishers, New York 1989

!King, Junior, Martin Luther *I Have a Dream: Writings and Speeches that changed the World* Harper San Francisco, New York 1992

*Milton, Joyce *Marching to Freedom: The Story of Martin Luther King, Jr.* Dell Publishing Co., New York 1987

*!Shuker, Nancy *Martin Luther King* Chelsea House Publishers, New York 1985